Music in Missions:
Discipling Through Music

T. W. Hunt

MUSIC in MISSIONS:
Discipling Through Music

BROADMAN PRESS
Nashville, Tennessee

© Copyright 1987 • Broadman Press
All Rights Reserved
4263-43
ISBN: 0-8054-6343-7

Dewey Decimal Classification: 266
Subject Heading: MISSIONS, MUSIC
Library of Congress Catalog Number: 86-28333
Printed in the United States of America

Library of Congress Cataloging-in-Publication Data

Hunt, T. W., 1929-
  Music in missions.

  Bibliography: p.
  1. Missions—Music. I. Title.
ML3000.H91   1987   264'.2   86-28333
ISBN 0-8054-6343-7 (pbk.)

Contents

Foreword 7

1. The Role of Music in Missions 11

2. The Missionary Musician 36

3. Communicative Method in Music Evangelism............................45

4. Principles of Training 60

5. Traditional Methodology in Music Missions.............................81

6. Indigenous Music...112

7. Indigenization 132

Epilogue 154

Appendix 157

Bibliography 176

Foreword

I have always felt that a book intended to help someone do something should be short and to the point. My philosophy collided with reality as I grappled with condensing some of the principles I had learned and having to leave others out in the writing of this book. Any chapter would make a hefty volume if treated adequately. It is a bit frustrating to desire to offer real help in real situations, but to realize that too much help discourages those seeking it. In the end, I attempted to compromise the various subjects by offering enough to be suggestive but not so much that I would be attempting to exhaust an inexhaustible subject.

The material for this book grew out of seventeen years of teaching a course in the use of music in missions at Southwestern Baptist Theological Seminary, Forth Worth, Texas. Those years saw considerable travel on five continents as I worked in conferences with music missionaries, worked on two sabbatical leaves as a music missionary in Spain, interviewed hundreds of missionaries, and discussed strategy with agency personnel and issues with missiologists. When I began teaching the course in late 1966, we mailed questionnaires to every missionary under appointment by the Foreign Mission Board of the Southern Baptist Convention. The return was nearly 57 percent—an astonishing response—indicating the level of interest and the enthusiasm for what music can accomplish in mission work. Since that time, I have supervised mailing of two other student questionnaires, and each time we have received an unexpectedly high

8   Music in Missions: Discipling Through Music

level of response. There has also been considerable dialogue and correspondence with missionaries and agency heads of twenty-eight other agencies which send music specialists to work in mission areas. This book attempts to synthesize results of the experiences of missionaries who were willing to talk about their failures and successes.

Because a mission philosophy will have bearing on any New Testament church, the book will be of interest to pastors and ministers of music. Their world is included in Christ's command, for the making of disciples is conditioned only by the word *going,*—an action word. The *where* is wherever the going is, the *what* is always discipling. It simply may not have occurred to some ministers that music can play a vital role in disciple making. The section on evangelism is intended to help evangelists and music evangelists, and I hope that the entire book will serve as a useful handbook for any home or foreign missionary.

The overall mission philosophy from which this book grew can only be grasped by reading the entire book, but the various chapters can also serve as reference material for those attempting any of the different musical activities described therein. The only technical chapter is chapter 4, and nonmusicians may skip that chapter unless they are grappling with the conceptual processes in diatonic music. Designed to be a handbook for disciplers, who might refer now to this section then to another, the book should be a helpful reference for anyone on mission for the Lord who wishes to use music in the task.

I consider missions to be the advance of Christianity and the main business of missions to be the making of disciples of Jesus Christ. Advance can occur in any situation where Christ is not the Lord of all persons in that setting; geographical proximity to a particular style of the practice of Christianity may have nothing to do with the need for "advance" in that sense. The drama is not geographical alone; it is a spiritual advance among people.

This book is not an ethnomusicology book, although ethnomusicology plays a major role in mission strategy. There is a great

Foreword

need for a Western missiologist to understand nonwestern music in greater depth, but there are also needs for surveys to determine what kinds of music urbanites might respond to in Seattle and Madrid. Ethnomusicology ultimately includes an understanding of the meaning of music, wherever that music is practiced, and missions includes reaching the unreached wherever they may be, whether they be "Christianized" or "hidden peoples."

The programs of the twenty-eight agencies with which I have had some communication embrace many kinds of musical specialization. Music missions includes an enormous variety of activity. Some missionaries using music effectively work in such sophisticated cities as Buenos Aires and Tokyo. Their approach must consider not only ethnomusicology but urban studies and demography. The music which people hear in urban areas is catholic and syncretistic and will likely include at least some which the missionary has heard before. Other missionaries work with rural peoples whose music may be entirely new to the missionary. These workers will need greater depth of understanding of ethnic principles. I believe that this is the first *general* book on music missions (not on ethnic Christian music). As a beginning effort, it would seem to be most helpful if it addressed as many missionaries as possible, wherever they may be working.

Music has always been an integral part of missions, just as it has been in Christianity. The principles set forth in this book could well be based on any period of Christian history. The rather enormous collection of material in my office files could furnish documentation from any year since 1966 for the principles stated here. I have chosen to use documentation covering a wide span of time. This will demonstrate the universality of some of the principles and will also show that music missions is not new. Many of the documents are missionary letters; some are statements by and in music mission conferences (Africa, Latin America, and Asia have had continent-wide Baptist church-music conferences); others derive from a variety of unclassifiable sources: general prayer letters, circular newsletters, and conversations long forgotten (if one would document a conversation).

I have chosen to use the word *music* occasionally as an adjective. Webster does not classify it as such, and yet defines *music box* and *music drama*. Generally, I tried to let the "ring" of the word in popular understanding guide me as to how a phrase might be understood. We could easily have both music missionaries and musical missionaries.

I am indebted to a host of godly missionaries who have influenced me greatly over these years of working with missions. I have not forgotten them, but who reads lists of names? What I have forgotten is which particular one, on a given occasion, said the thing that clicked as "right" and helped me get hold of a principle. There are hundreds of these, and they are the real heroes in God's army—the ones who got their hands dirty doing the work but remain unsung at home. My prayer is that God will reward them. It is because of them that this book is possible. It is my prayer that the book will influence others to go do God's work as they did.

1

The Role
of Music in Missions

Throughout its history, Christianity has been a singing religion. Christianity has developed a form more diverse and complex than any other religion in the world, and in a vast majority of its various manifestations music in one form or another is used extensively. Christianity has never been without music; it has often been said that Christianity without music is unthinkable.

Missions is the advance of Christianity, and from the beginning an extensive use of music in missions has characterized that advance. At the beginning of the mission story, Paul wrote his own mission fields instructions to sing with "melody in your heart to the Lord" (Eph. 5:19), "with grace in your hearts to the Lord" (Col. 3:16), and with "spirit, and . . . with the understanding also" (1 Cor. 14:15). William Carey sang a Bengali hymn, "Jesus, and shall it ever be,/A mortal man ashamed of Thee," at the baptism of Krishna Pal, his first convert, in Serampore in 1800,[1] and he also composed a hymn on the occasion of the translation of the New Testament into Bengali. The well-known Bagby family documented their own use of music in their work in Brazil, and the pioneer missionary Solomon Ginsberg wrote many original hymns in Portuguese as he traveled in evangelistic work in Brazil.[2] Ginsburg wrote:

> One source of good results was our own hymn book, called "Cantor Christao" [sic]. I started that book while in Pernambuco, even before becoming a Baptist. . . . The first one I ever translated into the Por-

11

tuguese language was that inspiring one: "Showers of Blessings." The native believers took to my hymns gladly, which encouraged me greatly. It did me good to hear them sing those beautiful Gospel songs in their homes, in the work-shops and even as they were walking along the streets.[3]

The pages of *The Foreign Mission Journal* during the early years of the work of the Foreign Mission Board of the Southern Baptist Convention abound with numerous examples of music being used very extensively as Southern Baptist missions were being extended. Mrs. Grace Boyd Sears reported on a summer Bible school held in Pingtu, China, in 1912:

Six sessions were held daily, as well as a Sunrise Prayer meeting, [and] four singing practices . . .

From 8 to 9 A.M. we had a singing lesson, using our newly adopted hymn-book; good progress was made as the Chinese are always enthusiastic over music. I wrote the tunes on the blackboard and they copied them into their hymn-books.[4]

J. J. Taylor of South Brazil reported on the conversion of two women who were drawn to Christ through music (only one of the accounts is given here):

[A formerly resistant woman] is to be baptized soon. Living neighbors to a family of believers out in the country, she, her husband and nephew, for a long time held aloof in great disdain and would have none of the religion of the "Protestants," till one night the believers, Daniel-like, threw open their windows toward the residence of these opposers, singing joyfully many of the beautiful hymns that they so love. Thus they conquered. The neighbors came out, listened, sauntered towards the place and finally came in and expressed a desire to hear more songs, and also to hear something read out of the Book.[5]

W. G. Bagby reported on open-air meetings in Santos, Brazil, in 1904:

Our songs always attract the multitude, and they came flocking around

The Role of Music in Missions

from all sides. The members of our band of converts were greatly cheered by this first attempt at open air preaching in Santos, and so last Sunday they eagerly joined me in another meeting in the same place, and this time fully three hundred persons soon crowded about us as we sang, and listened eagerly to the message of life.[6]

Since the appointment of large numbers of music missionaries beginning in 1951 and the establishment of seminary courses in music missions, missionaries have become even more conscious of the value of music as a tool for outreach, and new strategies to make the use of music more effective have been tried. Awareness has been heightened also by frequent articles in mission journals and music journals.

Missionaries report a large number of functions of music in missions. These may be divided into four general categories:

1. *Natural or characteristic functions inherent in music,* that is, those accomplishments in mission work owing their origin to the natural operation of music as it is allowed to function normally.

2. *Functions of music with various kinds of social groups,* or those functions possible because music tends to unify persons within groups and to appeal to common-interest groups. Music is the most social of the arts, and often it will reach an entire group at one time if addressed specifically to that group.

3. *Functions of music in missionary activity,* referring to those functions which enhance and enable the realization of the missionary purpose.

4. *Functions of music in the Christian life,* or those specific functions which touch on the individual and corporate growth of the believer(s).

Natural or Characteristic
Functions Inherent in Music

Music is one of the most characteristic expressions of humanity. Anthropologists report that it is universal. Music itself is not a universal language, but all tribes, clans, and nations have some sort of

14　　　　　　　　　　　Music in Missions: Discipling Through Music

music. It characterizes Bible life from Jubal (Gen. 4:21) to the singing hosts of Revelation. When Jesus was chiding the Jews for their lack of response, He used music as an example of an agency which demands response:

> "But to what shall I compare this generation? It is like children sitting in the market places, who call out to the other children, and say, 'We played the flute for you, and you did not dance; we sang a dirge, and you did not mourn'" (Matt. 11:16-17, NSB).

Christ was not directly speaking of music, of course, but in the comparison He implied a power which demands response. Most of the functions which follow are a paraphrase of the sum of several statements from different missionaries.

1. *Spiritual life generates song.* "Is any merry? Let him sing psalms" (Jas. 5:13). The evidence of experience and of history attest the inevitability of a "new song" wherever Christ penetrates a heart. This inevitability facilitates the outburst of indigenous song if new Christians are allowed the freedom to express their new faith naturally. Mrs. Donald Simms, who worked among the K'ekchi Indians of Guatemala, reported:

> We found, especially among new Christians, that singing is the first expression for their new-found joy in Christ following their public commitment. As a new believer, the Christian vocabulary is a new one, but immediate memorizing of hymns gives the earliest opportunity for them to witness. It is not unusual for a one- or two-week-old "babe in Christ" to sing a solo during testimony time.
>
> Until last Sunday (March 12, 1967) we had no musical instrument for our worship services in our little mission. With funds saved from various sources we bought, for $200.00, a portable pump organ. When we arrived at the service our people were so happy over the newly acquired organ that they sang almost every hymn they knew. The song leader would apologize for singing so much—and then announce another hymn![7]

2. *Music is a significant expression of culture.* Culture is the expression of

The Role of Music in Missions

all that is human. Each of the various people groups of the earth has its own unique personality, expressed in its music, its customs, its poetry, and its language. No aspect of human personality should be ignored as an avenue of approach; musical expression is one of the most significant and characteristic expressions of the pattern of culture. An indigenous hymnody is one of the first signs that Christianity itself is truly indigenous.

Universally, missionaries reporting on three questionnaires over more than a decade are enthusiastic about the power of music. H. B. Bickers, of Malawi, said, "Music is vital, as it is the one common expression readily understood and felt by all the people, regardless of language or education. It is a major key in developing new work."[8] Joan Varner spoke of the response in Brazil: "Brazilian people love music of all types and are always responsive to music well performed." L. B. Akins reported on Taiwan: "Music makes a great impact upon the Chinese, and many have been at least greatly influenced by music."

3. *Music functions as a mnemonic aid with texts.* Western culture is the most eye-minded culture in history; probably no other group of people relies more on visual memory. But even in the West, we are familiar with the ability to recall words of hymns or of any sung text. Glenn Boyd gave an example:

> In the early stages of our hymnal planning, Marilyn McMillan, faculty member of our seminary in Tanzania, Jeannine (my wife), and I had discussed setting Biblical texts to existing tribal tunes. I challenged a group of women, wives of pastor students, to set a list of the books of the Bible to a pre-existing tune. A class of Marilyn's finally worked out a setting, which became the first of a series of tribal tunes we used. . . . It facilitated memorizing the books of the Bible. They were thrilled that it was an easy way to memorize.[9]

4. *Music has a high value as a signal; that is, it has a speed factor in attracting attention.* The term *signal* is used in a technical sense; in communication, it is any agent which attracts attention (See chapter 3 under

16 Music in Missions: Discipling Through Music

"Frame."). Mrs. William L. Hashman III, of Japan, said, "In Japan, music . . . attracts more unsaved than any other facet of the church program." Pratt J. Dean, also of Japan, wrote, "Our Christmas music program drew two hundred. An average evening attendance is about thirty." Phillip Anderson, of the Philippines, declared, "[Music is] our best method of attracting people to services." Annie Hoover, in Japan, wrote:

> When we returned (from furlough) in June, 1966, three to six or seven were singing in the Sapporo choir. The church decided to have a special Christmas music program with Nomura-san directing. There were three choirs with a total of sixty voices; thirty were in the main choir, and they closed the program with the "Hallelujah Chorus." Three of the thirty have become Christians as a direct result of the music program. At least 163 were present, and this to my knowledge is a record attendance at the Sapporo Baptist Church since it was started in my living room in 1952 . . . Often we hear in a testimony "I came to hear the music" or "I returned because of the music." One of the leading deacons in Otaru came the first time to a Christian meeting to hear Sue Emanuel play the Hammond organ.

William R. O'Brien added a remarkable story from Indonesia:

> On a tour to west Java we were scheduled to sing in the city of Bogor. Baptists had never before entered this city, a beautiful mountain city located about thirty miles from the capital, Djakarta. . . . A Baptist family [missionary Avery Willis] had been asked to move there upon the completion of language study and open our first work. I told them that if the choir could be used as a wedge for public relations, as a tool to establish any kind of relationship . . . [to] feel free to use us. So we agreed to sing a concert on the Friday night preceding the first public worship service of this Baptist work.
>
> I had agreed that we would sing and leave immediately by bus in order to get into the city of Djakarta before the night curfew at eleven o'clock. [Willis called long-distance to tell us] that we must do two concerts in Bogor rather than one. . . . Avery explained that he had rented the largest movie theater (seating 800) and then had immediate-

The Role of Music in Missions   17

ly given out 2,000 tickets to insure a crowd. He had not been in Indonesia long enough to realize that 2,000 tickets meant he probably needed 2,000 seats. So when he learned what the public response was going to be, he urged us to do two programs. We agreed. We sang the first one at 6:00 [PM] to a full house—800 people. The choir sang for an hour and forty-five minutes, really "up" emotionally, because they realized what an impact they could have in this strategic city at the very beginning of Baptist work. The military leaders and the mayor of the city were there and gave us warm greetings. . . . [The second performance was] packed—about 1,000 people. . . .

The first public worship service was announced for the following Sunday. . . . The Willeses had the service in the living room of their home and they reported that over 100 people had packed into their living room. Two of them made professions of faith during that very first service. And so the choir felt that they had been a vital and integral part of planting seeds, of opening hearts, of tearing down barriers, and walls of misunderstanding and suspicion.[10]

5. *As a communicative channel, music facilitates the transmission and reception of certain kinds of information.* Not all the information we want to communicate denotes specific and limited fact; much is communicated through attitude. This will be discussed in chapter 3.

6. *Music is adaptable to almost any sphere of mission effort.* Among the innumerable activities enhanced by music, missionaries name student work, medical work, goodwill centers, television, associational meetings, school programs, and a Christian cultural center in Colombia. It is hard to imagine a mission activity which would not find good use for music.

Functions of Music with
Various Kinds of Social Groups

By its nature group singing requires such coordination that it tends to unify a group psychologically and spiritually. It expresses mutuality of purpose and of almost any common emotion; therefore, it is especially valuable in corporate worship. A culturally valid style will

18   Music in Missions: Discipling Through Music

also appeal to an entire group at the same time. It was a social expression in the Bible; in the story of the prodigal son, the joy at the prodigal's return was expressed by music: "Now his elder [brother] was in the field: and as he came and drew nigh to the house, he heard music and dancing" (Luke 15:25).

1. *Music often breaks the barrier against women's expression.* H. B. Bickers, in Malawi, explained:

> Normally in an African culture, it is very difficult to get women to express themselves in public because by their very culture they are shy and retiring. . . . when a woman is before a group it is very, very seldom that she will raise her eyes from the ground. It is very difficult to get women to stand up in front of a group and express anything.
>
> But the unique thing about it is the fact that they will sing. Where they will not speak to a group, they are willing, in a moment's notice, to stand up and sing. So once again you ask, "Does music help communicate the gospel?" Yes, it does, because music has broken through one of the oldest cultural barriers of the African people. It has allowed the women a way and an opportunity to express their testimony in front of men.[11]

2. *Music gives the reticent and the timid a personal expression.* This is true in all cultures, including churches in the West. Certain cultures, however, tend to emphasize reticence as a social grace, for example, the high cultures of the Orient. Christians in these cultures delight in their freedom to participate in group activities which do not single them out.

3. *It is especially valuable in reaching children.* H. B. Bickers, of Malawi, added to his observations:

> There is one more way in which music has been especially helpful in our work as missionaries here in Malawi—with the children. I suppose that children in every place like to sing . . . and the African children love to sing. Any place you go, in any village, you can begin to sing. . . . If you sing it twice, they can sing it from memory because they learn so quickly. The children learn very quickly through music.[12]

The Role of Music in Missions 19

The pages of *The Foreign Mission Journal* during the early years of Foreign Mission Board work contain a surprising number of references to children responding to music. In 1897, Mrs. W. P. Winn of Africa (no further identification is given) wrote of children singing, "They are never ready to quit, but sing with all their might several translations of Sankey's hymns."[13] A notice appeared in 1908:

> Many times the children in China take the gospel into places the missionary cannot enter. Those who are sent to the village schools carry home in their minds many Bible texts and now and then, when the children in America send them, such a bright beautiful card, with a Scripture text on it, that it is passed from hand to hand and the text read again and again by heathen as well as Christian neighbors. Then, as you pass down the streets, you may hear high childish voices singing a Christian hymn, that, whether they will or not, tells the story to the proud heathen who perhaps pass the missionary by.[14]

4. *It attracts population segments hostile to the gospel.* The tendency to erect barriers against preaching often disappears when music is the communicative vehicle. William R. O'Brien described an event which occurred in Indonesia during the Communist preparation for their attempted coup d'etat of 1965 (the coup failed):

> In May of 1965 the Baptist Seminary Choir was going to east Java on a four-day tour. As we were planning to sing in the city of Kediri, where we have located a large Baptist hospital, some pessimistic reports kept coming, saying something like this: "Don't come now. The Communist pressure is too strong. It would not be wise to come with an American conductor." But pastors and laymen who were faithful and concerned wrote me saying, "This is the time to come, for if we do not witness when the chips are down, we have no right to witness when things are going smoothly." So we went.
>
> The committee rented the largest movie theater in the city, seating about 1,200. That night as we prepared for the program in a little side room, the sixteen-seventeen-man committee met with us in prayer. I wish you could have heard them pray that night! . . . We sang the first

portion of the program and then one of the national pastors came to the microphone and preached for about ten minutes. This we did not usually do, because our publicity was pitched toward a night of music, and if the people came under the guise of entertainment, then left feeling they had been tricked, it would not have been good. But adequate preparation had been made in the publicity for this particular evening, so they were aware of what was going to happen.

The young man preached; we finished the concert with another forty-five minute section of music, and then he returned to the platform to extend a public invitation. I sat on the front row, not seeing what was happening behind me. The house lights were still out, but I could hear the shuffle of feet on the dirty concrete floor. When the invitation was closed some fifteen minutes later, . . . one of the national pastors said, "I believe we had about 150 public decisions tonight out of that 1,200 who were packed into the theater." And sure enough, there were, some fifty-six of these being first-time professions of faith. Within two months they had been assimilated into the life of local churches (not all Baptist). The choir left the next morning testifying and singing to each other about the joy they had experienced in coming into a very tense situation, filled with pessimism and love, singing the gospel, and experiencing that kind of response.[15]

5. *Musical activities organized around common-interest groups provide both appeal and incentive.* A factor that often expresses commonality in peer groups is music. Mrs. Hugh T. McKinley, of Zimbabwe, gave an example: "Several churches have been able to reach young people through a young people's choir." Doris Blattner confirmed the same pattern in Indonesia: "The choir is a means of enlisting young people, and is often the strongest organization for young people in the church." Chen-Kuang Chang, a national Chinese who is president of the Taiwan Baptist Seminary, said, "Most young people come to the church through the attraction of the choir program."[16]

6. *Music establishes the Christian group in the community.* The first music missionaries appointed by any agency were Mr. and Mrs. Donald (Violet) Orr by the Southern Baptist Foreign Mission Board on April 19, 1951, to teach in the Music Department of the International

The Role of Music in Missions 21

Baptist Seminary in Cali, Colombia. Orr's first terms were marked by persecution in pre-Vatican-II days, but he achieved a remarkable breakthrough in Cali in 1964. In his own words:

The influence of our music program has been felt all over the country, and we were invited to participate in a production of *Messiah* by the English-speaking community there [in Bogota]. The American ambassador was the bass soloist for their performance, and it was presented twice there for the English-speaking people, and also in the Colegio Americano for Spanish-speaking people. This concert was also presented on television, which is governed by the government of Colombia.

After the success of this undertaking in Bogota, we felt that we could accomplish the same thing in Cali, since we have a rather large international community there also. We began rehearsals, had a choir of sixty, made up of professors, dentists, doctors, Peace Corps young people, students, missionaries, businessmen and wives. The American Consulate personally "backed" this enterprise, and it was presented in the Municipal Theater (the local "opera house"). It was received with great acclaim, receiving effusive praise in newspapers and radio, and there were three direct outcomes from the performances, the one in the Municipal Theater (where there were tickets sold for the performance) and one free to the public in the First Baptist Church auditorium. These results were:

1. An invitation by the director of the theater to repeat the performance in January for many of the "musically elite" who had missed the performance.
2. An invitation by the Committee of the Annual National [Roman Catholic] Sacred Music Festival, to take place in Popayan (a very strong Catholic center) in February.
3. A "breakthrough" in public relations and "good will," by the request of the director of the University chorus to present a Protestant oratorio, "The Crucifixion" (translated into Spanish) in our First Baptist Church auditorium during Easter Week.

. . . It was our great joy to have the University Choirs present the oratorio "La Crucifixion" in our auditorium on Good Friday, and to see people attend a service in a Baptist church who would never have dared enter its doors, either to sing in it or to attend a service there, because of stigma, or prejudice. Never again would they have this reservation.[17]

It is believed that the news story covering this event the morning after its first performance contained the first time the word *Baptist* ever appeared in a Colombian newspaper.

Functions of Music in Missionary Activity

Although all the functions named by missionaries contribute in one way or another to the furthering of the Christian cause in mission areas, some are more specifically applicable to missions than others.

1. *Basic musical skills are indispensable to the normal and effective functioning of a missionary.* Missionaries must function in innumerable ways in which they would not function in comparable ministries at home. They must have multiple skills to function efficiently in societies furnishing fewer technical specialists (in any field). One of the skills all missionaries need is a rudimentary mastery of music basics. An unsigned questionnaire from Indonesia reported: "Often I have heard missionaries who do not feel they can carry a tune or who do not know one note from the other say, 'If I just had some *basic* knowledge of music it would help me so much.'" An unsigned questionnaire from Japan stated, "If you know music, you will be able to communicate through this medium at least two years before you will ever be able to communicate effectively by speaking, preaching, or teaching in Japanese." Darline Elliott, of Colombia, gave an experienced opinion: "Every male missionary should be able at least to direct congregational singing, and every woman should be able to play at least one musical instrument."

Advice given in 1897 still is applicable after many decades. Referring to a missionary teacher in a Christian school in Chin-kiang, China, W. W. Lawton wrote:

[Miss Mackenzie] makes them learn songs when she is with them; and in one week you should see the difference in their singing. I am no

The Role of Music in Missions

singing-master, but I am very glad I took dear Dr. Broadus' advice and listened to the singing in the Seminary. What would I do without that training now? It is at present needed as much as Greek or Hebrew. I often think of what I heard Dr. Bryan say in the home land—"We are singing Christ into the Chinese."[18]

2. *Music is a useful medium for the transmission and teaching of theological concepts.* The primary factor making music a useful vehicle for teaching is its mnemonic faculty—we remember better what we sing. Ambrose of Milan, Isaac Watts, and John Newton, to mention a few, infused a didactic function into their hymn writing. Hymns (for better or for worse) can be used to popularize theological concepts. Music also lends a persuasive leverage to the theology it is channeling. This capacity is potentially dangerous of course and demands integrity and perceptiveness on the part of musicians who serve the Lord.

3. *Church music education is especially magnetic in some areas.* Evelyn Owen, an accomplished missionary cellist in Japan, wrote:

> In Japan, because of the high level of music appreciation among the Japanese people, alongside a lack of opportunity to receive training in *Christian* music (and a resulting relatively undeveloped state of the music program in most churches), the opportunities in the future are unlimited.

Even in areas where music is a part of the school curriculum, parents welcome an opportunity to provide their children with church music education, although in some cases the family is not Christian. After studying church music in Southwestern Baptist Theological Seminary for a year, Nomura Hiroko established a program of children's choirs in Sapporo Baptist Church, Sapporo, Japan, and soon found that as news of her program spread, she had an entree into non-Christian homes into which even the pastor had not been able to obtain entrance.

One of the most outstanding graded choir programs outside the United States is in Oi-Machi Baptist Church, Tokyo, directed by

Rennie Sanderson Ohtani. These programs attracted not only children but their families. Mrs. Ohtani had a "music deacon" to assist her in the development of the program, and she chose leaders from the church to be responsible for the areas of congregational singing, choirs, instrumental music, training, publicity, and promotion.[19]

4. *In some countries, musical literacy is considered basic to a normal education.* Developed countries, such as those in Europe or the high cultures of Asia, have a highly literate population; the average Japanese has a remarkable knowledge of the history of Western music. Missionaries working in such environments are at a considerable disadvantage if they do not possess a modest acquaintance with Western art history as well as the national music. It could be argued that this circumstance is not a function of music. Still, unquestionably the inability to relate to the national on a plane which the national considers important places the missionary at a disadvantage. The existence of this kind of interest tells us something of the national interest in music.

5. *In other areas, such as most of Africa south of the Sahara, all people are expected to perform functionally and naturally in local styles, as well as in related styles.* The concepts of "musicality" and "unmusicality" do not exist in many parts of the world. These concepts are unique to the culture of the West which has produced a highly stratified musical society based partly on tastes, partly on education, and very little on actual musicality. This attitude assumes that "unmusical" persons will be unable to perform certain sophisticated musical tasks. John Blacking's comments are perceptive:

> "My" society claims that only a limited number of people are musical, and yet it behaves as if all people possessed the basic capacity without which no musical tradition can exist—the capacity to listen to and distinguish patterns of sound. . . . A producer's training in Western European culture must have taught him that not all people are musical, and that some are more musical than others. But his knowledge and experience of life lead him unconsciously to reject this theory. Capitalist dogma tells him that only a chosen few are musical, but capitalist

The Role of Music in Missions 25

experience reminds him that *The Sound of Music* was one of the biggest box-office draws of all time.[20]

In East Africa, for example, an "unmusical" member of a tribe would generally be considered an anomaly, a surprise, completely unexpected. All children sing naturally, and the complex rhythm of the drums is a part of their musical language from infancy.

These tribes will often have musical offices, at times designated by tribal tradition, but the idea of a nonperformer is foreign to their thinking. Missionaries have reported that a certain tribe might appear more or less sensitive musically than another tribe, but even in these cases the thought that a person might be *unable* to perform music is not a part of their outlook. The practical upshot of this is that music is a more integral part of the lives of these peoples than it is in the West, where many individuals go through a lifetime without benefit of music because they were told as a child that they were "unmusical."

In much of East Africa, music is such a part of all of life that there are songs, and even song styles, for the various life activities: sowing, reaping, canoeing, marrying, dancing, initiating, and so forth. Song is almost as much a part of their lives as language, and the idea of canoeing or marrying without music is very nearly unthinkable. It is no coincidence that the greatest success (among Baptist musicians) in the developing of indigenous styles today is found in these cultures. Music is as natural as birth or eating.

A significant degree of tribal interchange is going on in many of these areas, and many persons will be multilingual as well as "multimusical" (fluent in several different indigenous styles). Others will not have fluent musical expression in the other styles but will have a functional ability to distinguish styles. This is especially true where a trade language, such as Swahili, has become widely used. What would be considered in America as extraordinary talent and musical sensitivity is hardly noteworthy in such places.[21]

Functions of Music in the Christian Life

There must be good reason why Christians are commanded to sing in the Bible; this is one command (at least) which has been consistently kept and observed in all times and places! Without church music, there would scarcely be a history of music; without song, worship and fellowship would assume a format and style radically different from any form known today. Missionaries have designated eight functions of music in the Christian life which are useful in missions; no doubt these could be multiplied, but in the form given here they are at least suggestive.

1. *Music is a useful and effective medium for worship.* In the Bible, music is used to signify or anoint God's chosen vessels (1 Sam. 10:5), is associated with the promises of God (Isa. 51:3), signifies the presence of God (Ps. 32:7), and is repeatedly enjoined and used in Old and New Testament worship (1 Chron. 6:31-44, Matt. 26:30, etc.).[22] We are repeatedly told to "sing praise," "sing to the Lord," "sing a new song," and so forth. The use of all kinds of instruments, solos, choirs, and loud voices is encouraged. The Bible furnishes an almost embarrassing wealth of references detailing the music to be sung, instruments to be played, and the manner of performance in worship.

Both music and worship are spontaneous expressions of the new life in Christ our converts experience. The missionary may need to encourage their practice where cultural timidity causes slower development, but it is at least normal to expect music and worship to surface voluntarily. There also may be some awkwardness in the choice of music sung (a secular song, a song not germane to the service at hand, and so forth; see chapter 5), but treated unselfconsciously and naturally, the problem is usually solved easily.

2. *Christian musical expression sometimes supplants a heathen practice.* The radical demands of Christianity are no less severe in mission areas than they are to the practiced and growing disciple in North America: deny yourself, come out from the world, let the dead bury their dead, and so forth. New converts may have difficulty disassociating them-

The Role of Music in Missions

selves from practices connected with witchcraft, revelry, initiation, and other ancient customs.

But "When the unclean spirit is gone out of a man, he walketh through dry places, seeking rest, and findeth none. . . . Then goeth he, and taketh with himself seven other spirits . . . and they enter in and dwell there: and the last state of that man is worse than the first" (Matt. 12:43-45). The person, of course, should be filled with the Holy Spirit to avoid "the devil's vacuum," but God Himself uses music to represent the work of spiritual agencies (Ps. 42:8). Marion Fray, speaking of his service in Zimbabwe, illustrated the principle: "Music is effective around village fires as a substitute for traditional spirit dances." Music is one of the most effective agencies we have for filling the vacuum created as life-styles change. It is, in fact, an appropriate expression of the new life.

3. *Music enhances, deepens, and gives expression to Christian fellowship.* Both music and dance require coordination if performed corporately (this may partially explain why Africans cannot disassociate the concepts of dance and music). Few things are more jarring than a discordant note in a harmonization or an "out-of-sync" beat in the rhythm of a piece. The blending of harmony and synchronization of rhythm can be representations of spiritual unity. Even if a cultural area is already accustomed to harmony, they may not have known the thrill of Christian fellowship, and music can express that. H. B. Bickers said:

> Music has given them this opportunity to begin to think together. With music, they learn to work together, and so this set the stage for the next step in the development of the churches. It lays groundwork; it teaches them how to work together, so that we might in turn teach them how to work together in the areas of witnessing and teaching and preaching and the aspects of the church life.[23]

T. W. Ayers described a charming scene, played long ago (1908) but repeated quite often in mission situations, of the quick development of fellowship in Christ expressed in music. A "Dr. Willingham" had preached a sermon to dedicate a new church in Hwanghien,

28   **Music in Missions: Discipling Through Music**

China. Ayers describes the scene as Willingham left the city the following day:

> They were escorted through the city by more than one hundred native Christians.... When they reached the outside of the city, they stepped from in front of Dr. Willingham's shentza to the side of the road and began to sing "Hallelujah." . . . Then, as his shentza started off, the brethren, with trembling voices, sang "God Be With You 'Till We Meet Again." This was an occasion which neither Dr. Willingham or the brethren can ever forget.[24]

4. *Music encourages and heartens the Christian in discouraging circumstances.* The midnight song of Paul and Silas (Acts 16:25) is the first recorded instance in history of Christian music encouraging in seemingly straightened circumstances. An account in a journal from 1896 provides a remarkably similar story. The report concerned a "Mr. Diaz" who had been imprisoned on the pretext that he gave medicine to Cubans.

> Men came and put additional bars in the windows, knock and hammer in the court-yard, and seem to be preparing a scaffold. He thinks his time to die has come, and begins to sing. His brother in the next cell joins in the song. They are told to stop—they must not speak; but they will not stop; they can but die. While they sing, like Paul and Silas, the doors are opened, and they are free. They hastened to the church, where the members were gathered, and walked in among them. There they stayed, praising God, until twelve o'clock.[25]

This ability of music to encourage has been turned into a science in the twentieth century. Music therapy has made great strides in perfecting techniques for helping the mentally distressed with music, but the practice is at least as old as David, for it is documented in the Bible in the account of David's ability to soothe the raging Saul with his harp (1 Sam. 16:23). We tend to "catch" the mood of song; Muzak has made a science of elevating moods, relieving exhaustion, encouraging spending, and more. There is danger in that this property of music can be used to manipulate, but the very fact that the capaci-

The Role of Music in Missions 29

ty to encourage is a natural outworking of some kinds of music indicates that God intended it to be a blessing. Missionaries can take advantage of this property for themselves as well as for their work. Many missionaries carry a large supply of Christian records for the personal encouragement they provide.

5. *Music integrates the Christian message and orientation with daily life.* There is no evidence in the Bible that God intended a division of the sacred from the secular; the division He intended was the holy from the unholy. Music is one tool Christians can use to sanctify their everyday lives. In some cultures, music is always associated with working, playing, and so forth (as opposed to the Western idea of music independent of activity). In much of Africa, music is thought of as something to *do* (as opposed to the Western idea of something to *listen* to). In those cultures in which the concept of music cannot be separated from the activities of life, music lends special power to the witness of (sacred) message by its very permeation into every area of secular life. Music, like Christ Himself, is always there. William L. Jester, of Nigeria, said flatly, "Music is such a vital part of African daily life that the church could not exist without it."

6. *Music functions as a stabilizing element in the lives of new believers.* This function relates to numbers 4 and 5 above: it encourages, and it is always there. Eva Sanders illustrated this faculty in a charming story from Nigeria:

> Back in the late twenties there was a little boy named Akin being raised by his heathen grandmother. She told him never to have anything to do with Christians and encouraged him to go outside the church during Sunday School and throw rocks at the lizards on the church walls. He enjoyed this sport. The sidesman went out and invited him in, so he ran away.
>
> However, the children had sung a hymn that caught his ear—not the words, but the tune. He returned the next Sunday to rock lizards. The children were singing the same song, and this time he listened more carefully. Again he was invited in, and again he ran away. This continued for weeks, and not once did the sidesman rebuke him. He says

30   **Music in Missions: Discipling Through Music**

now that he saw that this man was different from other people he knew. They sang the same song every Sunday, and it was like a magnet to him.

Finally, he went in and sat on the back seat so that he could get the words, but when one of the Christians approached him, he ran out. Still, he was always there to hear the song. He began to enjoy others, and gradually moved up until he was one of the children in the Sunday School class. He gave his heart to Christ and became a faithful witness.

He was helped by a missionary who paid his school fees and went through high school. He loved singing more than anything else in the school, and was one of a band that would go out to preach on Saturday afternoons and Sunday. He was excellent at teaching the children songs.

There was a cinema (movie house) across the street from his dormitory; a false prophet rented it at times and held services there. Akin would listen across the fence, and sometimes he would slip over there. We did not know about this until one day I was teaching "The First Noel." As usual, I explained the meaning of each line, and used scripture for each line if possible. When I explained that "Noel" meant "Good News," it stirred him up! After the service he came, and was very angry. He said he had learned that song in English before and loved it because it said, "No Hell."

It was most difficult to dissuade him from what he had learned across the street. He went through a hard period of doubt and sorrow, but with his love for music, he found comfort in the hymns. It was these that brought him back to his senses. Today he is a strong Baptist teacher, still in the choir, and helping others to learn hymns of faith.

7. It furnishes the Christian community a common, shared opportunity to witness. Many are fearful of witnessing alone, and choirs provide them with an opportunity to begin witnessing in less-intimidating situations. Mary Frank Kilpatrick wrote of some students in Nigeria:

> I do not know music, but I work with a choir of Baptist students in the university. Recently I took them on a tour to put on a program in six of our Baptist high schools and colleges. We put it on for a total

The Role of Music in Missions

of around 2,000 students. The university students were thrilled with this opportunity to witness.

8. *Music attracts the talented and provides outlets for believers with leadership abilities.* Music is very democratic; it belongs to the gifted and ungifted alike. Still, superior accomplishment in music is usually associated with unusual mental endowment. Those in leadership normally have a strong affinity for musical excellence and are drawn to musical programs. John H. McTyre wrote of one of his churches in Chile:

> Through the Christmas carol sing and the annual choral worship program in the church where I directed last term, the church came to be known as "the church with the choir!" Because of the choir program several with leadership qualities have been directly won to the Lord. One young man became the Sunday School superintendent, and his wife became a teacher.

And More . . .

This list of twenty-five functions is not exhaustive. The power of music finds expression every day in the world of mission and on the pages of history in ways far beyond mortal imagination because the work it accomplishes is divine. The limit is not human imagination but divine imagination—which is unlimited. A lovely report of the healing power of music appeared in the pages of *The Foreign Mission Journal* of 1899; an unnamed missionary had written a first-person report of her weekly boat visit to the Chinese village of Yadang:

> As soon as the boat stops in front of her house, I hear little Ah-lin calling me as she runs down the stone steps to the water. This little girl is about five years old, but until this year had hardly spoken a word, so that her friends began to fear she was dumb. She heard well, and understood all that was said to her, was a bright, lively child, but would not utter a word.
>
> All of a sudden she began to sing one day as she was in a little group of children whom I was teaching to sing a hymn, calling the words distinctly, and carrying the tune without mistake. She seemed delight-

32   Music in Missions: Discipling Through Music

ed with her acquirement, and wanted to learn another and another, until she knows quite a number by heart now. Her tongue was loosened with this first effort to sing, and now she talks just like any other child.[26]

The highest expressions of joy in the Christian life often come with song. F. M. Edwards described a baptismal scene in Brazil in 1908:

> One of those baptized is a very large man, and it did our hearts good to see him come out of the water and hear him singing at the same time, "Seguirei," which means "I will follow." While the water was dripping from his baptismal garments he and one of the deacons, another large man, fell on each other's necks and wept like children. It was a blessed time of rejoicing.[27]

Both the experience of history and the mandate of Scripture dictate the use of music in missions. Many missionaries have chosen to study music fundamentals after arriving on their field, and many nationals have found service through music when other doors were closed. Nomura Hiroko, a Japanese national converted from Sokka Gakkai Buddhism, taught herself to play the piano well enough to accompany congregational singing in only nine months. The story is an old one. V. I. Masters recorded a similar incident in Cuba in 1913. A Cuban missionary, Primo [sic] Navarro, with the Home Mission Board of his national Cuban Baptist Convention, discovered the need of music in his work:

> Recently he has taken to studying music, so that he may play the organ at his mission stations. At not one of them is there anyone to perform on the modest instrument that Brother Navarro desires to use to add to the harmony of worship in song. In fact, it is said that most of the people never heard an organ before the missionary came.
>
> Two months ago, when Superintendent McCall, of the Cuban missions, last saw Primo Navarro, the missionary was rejoicing on account of his progress in mastering the mysteries of pressing the organ keys in a way that would make harmonic sound. He said he could play two hymns with one hand. A month later he reported through the mails

The Role of Music in Missions

to the Superintendent with almost child-like gladness that he had now become *able to play eight hymns with both hands,* and had won for his work an organ a good woman had promised on condition he would master the thing.

When Navarro was bantered for his studious assiduity while he was practicing on the organ, with a voluminous by-product of plaintive and unarticulated wails from the reeded instrument, he replied:

"A great many play for pleasure. I must learn to play of necessity, for this thing is an absolute necessity in my work."[23]

Our choice, if we are to be effective missionaries, is not *whether* we will use music in our work. Our choice is *how* we will use it: effectively, efficiently, spiritually, or slovenly and carelessly. It remains to find those "handles" which make music work for us in the service of bringing this world to Christ.

Notes

1. "Program for December, 1902," *The Foreign Mission Journal,* Dec. 1902, 191. *The Foreign Mission Journal* was the organ of the Foreign Mission Board of the Southern Baptist Convention in the late nineteenth and early twentieth centuries.

2. T. W. Hunt, "Music in Missions," *Encyclopedia of Southern Baptists,* vol. 3 (Nashville: Broadman Press, 1971), p. 1859.

3. Solomon L. Ginsburg, *A Wandering Jew in Brazil* (Nashville: Sunday School Board, Southern Baptist Convention, 1922), pp. 122-123.

4. Mrs. Grace Boyd Sears, "Pingtu Summer Bible School," *The Foreign Mission Journal,* Oct. 1912, pp. 110-111. Many of these reports in the *Journal* were letters, and the by-line was given with title.

5. J. J. Taylor, "Trophies of the Gospel," *The Foreign Mission Journal,* Apr. 1912, p. 303.

6. W. B. Bagby, "Lengthening the Cords and Strengthening the Stakes," *The Foreign Mission Journal,* July 1904, p 34.

7. These functions were originally assembled and collated from the responses of missionaries to a questionnaire in 1966, mentioned in the Foreword. They have been revised by other questionnaires, by interviews with many missionaries, and by unsolicited suggestions from time to time in various conferences and colloquia. For example, the All-Africa Conference on Church Music held in Brackenhurst Baptist Assembly in November of 1981 reviewed the functions and suggested the addition of number five under "Functions of Music in Missionary Activity." All quotations not documented otherwise in the following section of this chapter are by missionaries who were

34   **Music in Missions: Discipling Through Music**

under appointment in 1966 by the Foreign Mission Board of the Southern Baptist Convention. Since all are from the same questionnaire, no further documentation will be provided for those responses. Unless indicated otherwise, the quotation is from a response to that first questionnaire. The respondents were not asked to identify themsleves by name in that questionnaire, but many volunteered that information. Names cited in this section were given at that time; where no name was given, the citation is given by the country of its origin. Most respondents did not date their responses—date was not asked—but all letters and questionnaires cited were between December, 1966, and March, 1967. Because there were approximately twelve-hundred replies to the questionnaire, it would be impossible to cite the many effective statements and insights furnished by it.

8. The quotations from H. B. Bickers are all from a tape received in Fort Worth in February, 1967, about music work in Malawi. His tape was Bickers's response to the questionnaire.

9. Glenn Boyd, "Indigenous Tunes in Swahili," *Missionary Notes,* No. 6, Sept. 1975, p. 8. *Missionary Notes* was a brief attempt at an exchange of information between music missionaries; it was published between 1971 and 1977.

10. William R. O'Brien, "Music Missions in Indonesia," 1973, unpublished monograph written for the Music in Missions class at Southwestern Baptist Theological Seminary, 1973, p. 3.

11. Bickers, tape.

12. Bickers, tape.

13. "Correspondence," *The Foreign Mission Journal,* July 1897, p. 47.

14. "The Children and the Gospel in China," unsigned article, *The Foreign Mission Journal,* October 1908, p. 126.

15. O'Brien, "Music Missions," p. 4.

16. A number of outstanding national musicians were also asked to respond to the questionnaire in 1967. Dr. Chang holds a Doctor of Musical Arts from Southwestern Baptist Theological Seminary in Fort Worth, Texas.

17. Donald L. Orr, "Music at Work on the Mission Field in Colombia," report presented to the joint meeting of Southern Baptist seminary faculties with Southern Baptist Sunday School leaders, Nashville, Tennessee, 19 Aug. 1965.

18. W. W. Lawton, "Correspondence," *The Foreign Mission Journal,* Apr. 1897, p. 387.

19. Rennie Sanderson Ohtani, "The Church Music Program at Oi Machi," monograph written for the Music in Missions class, Southwestern Baptist Theological Seminary, 1966.

20. John Blacking, *How Musical Is Man?* University of Washington Press, Seattle, 1973, pp. 8-9.

21. Glenn Boyd has stated that he once asked Manasseh Mutsoli, an outstanding Kenyan composer, how he composed and how he taught his choir sections their parts before he learned staff notation. Mutsoli replied that he "thought the music in his head" and then met with each section individually to teach them the part he had "thought" for them!

22. These references are only examples. The author has prepared an outline, "Func-

The Role of Music in Missions 35

tions of Music in the Bible," which attempts to list every passage in the Bible which treats music. The passages are almost countless.

23. Bickers, tape.

24. T. W. Ayers, "North China Paragraphs," *The Foreign Mission Journal*, Mar. 1908, p. 283.

25. "Sunday, 3 P.M." [Report of the Eighth Annual Meeting, Women's Missionary Union, Southern Baptist Convention, Chattanooga, May 8-11, 1896], *The Foreign Mission Journal*, June 1896, p. 79.

26. "Some Chinese Children," *The Foreign Mission Journal*, Aug. 1899, p. 90.

27. F. M. Edwards, "Itinerating in Brazil," *The Foreign Mission Journal*, Oct. 1908, p. 114.

28. V. I. Masters, "A Human Interest Story," *The Foreign Mission Journal*, Mar. 1913, p. 281.

2

The Missionary Musician

Missionary Musicians and Music Missionaries

This century has seen the expansion of mission methodology to allow vocational specialists in many fields to use their vocation as a means of outreach, and sometimes even as a means of getting into a country. The list of new vocations being used in mission methodology would be almost endless: agriculture, avaiation, communications, accountants, and so forth, not to mention the technical specialists in the sciences and arts.

Many great musicians of history—J. S. Bach, Felix Mendelssohn, and Ralph Vaughn-Williams, for example,—have proved that they could also be great children of God. But the last century has seen specific concern with evangelism and missions becoming a part of the very identity of some church musicians. Evangelists since D. L. Moody have used church musicians such as Ira Sankey, Phillip Bliss, and Cliff Barrows, whose commitment to Kingdom advance is beyond question. The modern music mission movement has produced dozens of musicians who became effective missionaries. Evangelism, commitment, spirituality, mission mindedness—these should be the hallmark of a genuine music ministry, whether it be in Dallas, Philadelphia, or Bangkok.

The first and primary reason for developing mission-mindedness in the Music Ministry is that we are Christians—not more Christian than the church ball team, or less Christian than the Sunday School. We can

36

no more assign degrees of Christianness than we can say that Texas is more American than Georgia. The Great Commission applies equally to the bell choir and to the church staff.[1]

Music specialists have ranked as the largest number among new vocational appointments since the early 1970s.[2] However, God did not wait until the twentieth century to send musicians to the mission field! History is replete with records of musicians who functioned as outstanding missionaries. No one knows how many missionaries are working currently in varying degrees in the field of music, but the number must be beyond imagination. If Christianity without song is unthinkable, then anywhere there is Christianity we should expect to find musicians. One encounters large numbers of missionaries highly qualified by training and talent who are not known as music missionaries but who make invaluable contributions through music in missions, both home and foreign. These persons have the same opportunities and the same frustrations as the specialists who go by the name *music missionary.*

However, it would be helpful to define just what a music missionary is to facilitate our discussion. For our purposes music missionaries meet four qualifications. (1) They are first and foremost *missionaries,* called to win the lost, to disciple converts, and to nurture national churches. (2) The primary area of their mission assignment is music,[3] although, like any missionary, they will be active in most phases of the work of their mission and accept nonmusical assignments as one of the privileges and obligations implicit in their appointment. (3) They are qualified by formal training for professional work in church music and normally are experienced in church music work before appointment.[4] (4) The majority of their missionary activities are musical ones. This last falls farthest short of being a rule; in fact, hardly any specialist can devote his energies to one speciality alone on the mission field.

That large host of additional missionary musicians—those for whom music is a secondary responsibility as opposed to those whose primary assignment is music—include many varying degrees of involvement and training. What really matters is that missionaries devote their peculiar talents and education to the purposes of the missionary enterprise, and that they be perceptive and imaginative enough to recognize the tremendous potential of music in mission strategy. We are limited only by the imagination to follow the Holy Spirit.

The Human Problems of Missionary Musicians

The first and primary requisite of a music missionary, or any missionary, is a divine call to missions. However, once that issue is settled, other considerations disturb many potential missionary candidates. A recurring question among young musicians when first confronted with the possibilities of a vocation in music missions is: "Would I be able to find fulfillment in music missions?" This question may reflect little more than the maturity of the one asking it, but it may also be a valid area of concern somewhat clouded by a vague but romantic notion that music as a career somehow satisfies certain highly personal needs that will not be met by other activities.

The notion is not pure illusion, for persons shall, indeed, not live by bread alone. We also shall not live by knowledge or accomplishment. We can only live through the Word of God, and that rich Word comes to us in multifarious ways because we are multiplex. God has graciously provided us with aesthetic sensibilities that round out our personalities and make us fully *human.* There are many things people say and hear best through music. But "music" is a very general concept, including many styles (or "languages") and many types of activity, and it is in the way in which these various activities "fulfill" us that confusion appears.

Also the dream of professional fulfillment is by no means limited to musicians as vocational specialists. Missionaries, like other people, hope to find both some degree of professional "fulfillment" along with the satisfaction of realizing the will of God in their lives. Inevi-

The Missionary Musician

tably, some professional frustrations, especially in areas of technical specialization, will emerge in any sphere of missionary activity.

A Sense of Identity

I once knew a missionary (with an agency I prefer not to identify) in Spain who preferred not to admit that she was an American. She refused to speak English, even in the company of American missionaries (and she spoke very good Spanish). She felt somehow that becoming a good missionary meant a denial of all that made her American. It is indeed highly commendable to master the language and customs of those we are trying to reach; it is praiseworthy to immerse oneself in the culture we are going to live in. Yet there is a logical contradiction in the supposition that being an American prevents one from functioning fluently in a Spanish culture. Denial of one's background is not the way to learn to function in a different milieu. Such denial puts one into a false role, and that will always produce frustration.

The missionary, true, can never return to the simplicity of life prior to learning another language and culture, but neither can one repudiate one's own past. When one rejects one's past, his or her sense of identity is destroyed as all the moorings of the old identity become meaningless. We do not secure our identity by destroying it and replacing it with another. We anchor to something—our past, the future, or both. Without an anchor we are orphans. Missionaries are new things, amalgams who are greater than the parts that went into their creation. They are probably better able to minister in their peculiar roles than they would have been without their acculturated mentality. Missionaries would do well to memorize Psalm 139: God gives us our birth, our spiritual life, and our calling. Under the lordship of Christ, we assume our ministry in His strength, neither denying our own identity nor refusing to absorb the new.

A realistic approach to vocational choice includes the fact that many professional frustrations are not a consequence of geography alone. Just what is it that young musicians want from their lives in music? What do they mean when they ask for "fulfillment?" The usual meanings include technical competence (attained in training and maintained and perfected by continued practice), the opportunity to hear (Western) music well performed (along with the connotative "meanings" associated with their particular background of Western music, far more satisfying than they realize until they are deprived of that music), and professional success. In short, they want to be good musicians, and they want to be known for that.

The young student almost invariably begins with an unrealistic standard for each of these goals—which is not entirely uncommendable. With regard to technical competence, one's criterion may be that of the professional artist. In point of fact, only a tiny fraction of musical aspirants attain such levels of artistry, and a smaller percentage of these attain enough professional success to support themselves economically. If success means fame and wealth, only a few attain it.

In recent years, vocational guidance counselors with their varieties of tests have enabled students to be more realistic about the promises of their careers. The music industry has expanded, so musicians have a wider choice of professional activity than ever before. If interest, ability, or determination preclude a performing career, the musician may find fulfillment in teaching, but many of the satisfactions of such work will not be specifically musical. Would-be composers may devote a major part of their work to arranging. Nevertheless a common complaint among American musicians is that their work is not fulfilling.

The other side of the coin is that many missionary musicians *have* realized unquestionable musical fulfillment specifically in their work as missionary musicians. Their choirs, their students, their hymnals, and their programs are monuments of professional achievement, requiring at times the highest level of musicianship.

Nevertheless, these achievements are often won at the expense of enormous labor, faithful self-giving, and seemingly infinite patience. Professional frustrations are to be found anywhere in the world in all vocations. The principal difference resulting from geography is

The Missionary Musician

one of degree, and that degree of difference is considerable—so considerable that many candidates for foreign missions should rule themselves out if musical fulfillment is more important than the missionary calling. Not only are there differences of degree, there are also differences in kind—differences which are reflections of culture and economic or political conditions.

The frustrations are as many and as varied as the locales. One obstacle every missionary musician will encounter is a lack of time for practice and personal development; he or she will also often lack musically challenging opportunities. A common problem for some is the very great length of time required to develop their programs and disciples. This, in turn, means that musical aspects such as choral tone or sharp performance (by Western standards) are also slow to develop. Because of differing levels of literacy, missionary musicians will find themselves working on lower levels of musical skill until they have developed among their constituency a working base of musical understanding. Maintenance of instruments becomes frustrating if pianos and organs are used.

Furthermore, in many mission situations, missionaries will have new and additional musical skills and concepts to study and learn (which, of course, may also be a specifically musical satisfaction). Those working in pioneer areas will need at least a modicum of ethnomusicology, which may be a new discipline for some. We cannot say that they will need greater spiritual insight and maturity than their counterparts at home, but lack of either will compound their frustrations. Without a solid grasp of their own identity and purpose, they will lack the essential fruit of the Spirit named by the first great Christian missionary in Galatians 5:22-23.

The same stateside musicians who are likely to overcome their problems will be the ones who can do it in mission work. The spiritual requisites are far more essential than the professional qualifications. The first, of course, is faith. Missionaries cannot function if they cannot trust God for what they need. The frustrations will be easier also if they can prayerfully adopt an attitude of servanthood

42   Music in Missions: Discipling Through Music

(Phil. 2:7). A third area will be the fulfillment that comes with the acquisition of new skills and concepts. These three areas are essential for a sense of self-identity in any kind of pioneer work: faith, servanthood, and growth.

Another problem surfaces when missionaries have no goals. A lack of goals leads to the frustration of retrogression. There can be no lack of potential goals on the mission field; there will always be new talent to find, new prospects to disciple, new hymnals to publish, new music to make available, and so forth. Finally, a problem which occasionally develops for missionaries is that of envy: the successful minister of music back home or the spectacular missionary in the next country or the next town. This leads to bitterness, the crippler for all Christian workers. Every unresolved problem leads to a crippling frustration.

Many areas for continuing personal development have been suggested by successful missionaries; the following is a condensation into seven:

1. Family relationships. The family becomes immeasurably more important in mission areas. The missionary can develop many family projects: music in the family, family devotions together, activities together, and so forth. The most successful and long-lasting missionaries have the most successful family life.

2. Mission relationships. The extended family is much more "family" overseas than in the United States. It is the custom in many missions for all "missionary kids" to call all adult members of the mission by the family name of "aunt" or "uncle."

3. National relationships. These should be natural, not forced. The missionary musician has advantages in the cultivation of national relationships—one can sing in the civic chorus (for example, Bill Ichter in Rio de Janeiro); one almost universally can find a door open by virtue of the universal love of music.

4. Language proficiency. Here again missionary musicians have advantages—they are accustomed to careful listening; they will memorize hymns quickly, etc. They can also: read and memorize

The Missionary Musician   43

Bible passages (they need to learn how the national Bible states various concepts and propositions anyway!), study the national poetry, listen to recordings, make lists of idioms, and so forth. It would be helpful to read the Bible through in the new language; they know the meanings of many verses already and will be surprised at how quickly they can recognize familiar passages when these are cited in their new language.

5. Bimusicality, or freedom to express oneself in a second musical language. Bimusicality achieves the same goal in music that bilinguality does in language and is one of the surest inroads into the confidence of the nationals. See chapter 7.

6. The mind of Christ. If one is a Christian, one already has the mind of Christ (1 Cor. 2:16) but may lack "handles" in expressing it. It is the servant mind.

7. One's own mission work. It should be professional, spiritual, and competent.

In the end, the most vital and fulfilling satisfactions for missionary musicians will not lie in musical or professional qualifications. These are likely to be realized to some degree, but their attainment is only incidental. The central purpose and the ultimate satisfaction of music missions lies in bringing men and women to a saving knowledge of Jesus Christ and discipling them. It is a missionary purpose, awesome in its responsibility. Similarly, the greatest problems lie not in the frustrations, many and varied though they may be. Our most serious problems are not those which frustrate the schedule or the program; rather, they are those which threaten the work of discipling.

The musical competence required for mission work should be of the highest level. The music missionary or the missionary musician is not *less* a musician; he or she is *more* a missionary. Donald Orr has said:

> The challenge and the joy of being the instrument through which God conveys the first musical grasp and participation for many of these people is a tremendous sense of satisfaction. . . . We are constantly too

44   Music in Missions: Discipling Through Music

busy to be able to perfect our own performing ability. This is the main thing we have had to sacrifice, but we are "expendable," and our main purpose is to *serve,* not to have a sense of satisfaction in our own prowess!! . . . We know that God is blessing every effort and that He is right ahead of us, preparing the *way, hearts, and means* to His glory![5]

And herein lies the open secret to the missionary musician's greatest source of fulfillment: it is a unique privilege to be the instrument through which God transmits His glory, and this in a special way. The music missionary's greatest joy is the glory of God.

Notes

1. T. W. Hunt, "A Musician's Response to World Missions," chapter 6 of *Bold Mission Music Handbook: A Music Director's Guide to Evangelism,* ed. Dan Johnson (Nashville: Convention Press, 1982), p. 78.

2. Music missionary appointments by the Foreign Mission Board of the Southern Baptist Convention have ranked second or third in number for several years. However, many of those working primarily in music are teachers in educational institutions, and are officially classified as "teachers" rather than "music missionaries."

3. The vocabulary used here is that of the Foreign Mission Board of the Southern Baptist Convention. Missionary are *appointed* in the United States but *assigned* to a specific work and place by their mission overseas. The term *mission* refers to all the missionaries in a given country; the term *station* refers to a locality within the country.

4. Usually the requirement of the Southern Baptist Foreign Mission Board is that they complete a master's degree in church music at a Southern Baptist seminary, which is to include at least twenty hours in theology (in some cases, these are taken subsequent to the finishing of the Master's), and have two years of experience in music work in a local church.

5. Letter to the author, 7 Sept. 1967.

3

Communicative Method in Music Evangelism

Music, Message, and Witness

The Bible is rich in references to the use of music. In the New Testament, it is used as an expression of faith (Acts 16:25), of joy (Jas. 5:13), and for worship (Revelation, *passim*). It is possible that the injunctions to sing in Ephesians 5:19 and Colossians 3:16 refer to differing emphases, both in their wording and in their context. The Ephesian passage follows an injunction to be filled with the Spirit and is coupled with thanksgiving; there the wording is specifically, "Singing and psalming with your heart to the Lord" (*adontes kai psallontes te kardia humon to kurio*). It is often translated, "Singing and making *melody* in your heart to the Lord" In Colossians, the injunction is in the context of teaching and admonishing (a word which can be as severe in meaning as "warning"); there the wording is, "Singing with *grace* in your hearts to God" (*en te chariti adontes en tais kardiais humon to Theo*).The emphasis in Colossians is slightly more horizontal; and the teaching and admonishing, in this context, is to be done "with grace."

If music is a communicative vehicle as well as a means to personally express spiritual joy, community, and praise, then we may expect the divine genius to have provided inherent communicative advantages in music. Ambrose, Watts, Newton, and many others deliberately infused a didactic function into their hymn writing. A communicative thrust is incidentally coupled with singing in Hebrews 2:12: "I will declare thy name unto my brethren, in the midst of the church will I sing praise unto thee." The Hebrew practice of parallelism associates "declaring His name" with "singing." Romans 15:9 even implies proclamation: "And that the Gentiles might glorify God for his mercy; as it is written, For this cause I will confess to thee among the Gentiles, and sing unto thy name." In the latter passage, Christ is a "minister of the circumcision" for two purposes: (1) to confirm the promises made to the Hebrew fathers, and (2) that the Gentiles might glorify God. Interestingly, it is in connection with the second that singing is mentioned.

In the light of such specific biblical directives, therefore, missionary musicians and anyone committed to evangelism should bring to musical outreach a method as articulate and even as adroit as homiletical specialists have applied to preaching. Effective evangelists have long utilized music, often very well, but the efforts are also at times diffuse and lack message. That God has blessed musical witness so abundantly is evidence of a potential perhaps not yet amply realized.

The constraint of the Great Commission is as binding on the music evangelist as it is on any Christian. If the work is done well, the receptors of our message will continue the chain by responding and assuming their own responsibility to evangelize, and they will be responding in their own culture as a natural communicator of Christ. If this chain involved every Christian, spiritual reproduction would be prolific at least in the same measure as physical reproduction.

We reproduce by communication. We are the agent of the Holy Spirit, communicating Christ to those to whom the Holy Spirit wants to give birth. In terms of communication, the evangelist is the *initiator*, a Christian who assumes the responsibility of providing information on Jesus Christ and His salvation to a non-Christian. The initiator's task is to translate the gospel into meaningful terms for another human mind, a *receptor*, a non-Christian targeted by the initiator as a prospect for the gospel on the basis of some apparent readiness to receive, understand, and accept data about Jesus Christ. The initiator must bear in mind that his data may not be immediately meaningful

Communicative Method in Music Evangelism

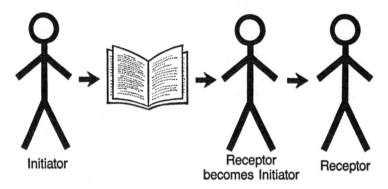

Figure 1. Chain of transmission of message

to the receptor. The receptor must grasp what the initiator is talking about (or singing about); he must receive the information, sort it out, put it into the framework of his own mentality and background before he can even understand that the gospel demands acceptance of its reality and its terms. This action is called *decoding;* decoding is the process of receiving information, deciphering it, and reacting to it positively or negatively.

Therefore the initiator must give careful thought and prayer to the transmission of the message, keeping in mind the receptor's problem of decoding whatever the initiator conveys. The initiator is concerned with the message and with the prospect's reception of it. The message will have two main aspects—the data or information itself, and the frame or the vehicle which carries the message.

Our information is a Person and the data which surrounds His work for us, that is, all data that is necessary for a valid, permanent commitment to Jesus Christ as Savior and Lord. In terms of communication, a group of data to be transmitted is conceived as a *code.* A code is a group of related facts, arranged in a sequence comprehensible to a receptor. For us, this data includes sin, God's loving intentions, His provision through the Person of Christ, and the purpose of the cross (but not necessarily a full understanding of atonement, with all its ramifications).

The *frame* is far more important than most evangelists realize. The frame is the vehicle chosen to carry and enhance data. It might be a song or a sermon, a poem or a tract, a chalk talk or a concert, a drama or a multimedia presentation. It is what Marshall McLuhan called the "medium."

McLuhan's famous dictum that the medium is the message may provide valuable clues to an operational method.[1] As a matter of fact, from biblical perspective, McLuhan's point of view may state most accurately the divine principle: Christ Himself is the Information we are seeking to communicate, and we—whatever we may be and however we may act—are the embodiment of the divine information that God has chosen to entrust with the commission of the good news.

Our command tells us that we are to be witnesses. We are not reporters. What is the difference? A reporter and a witness differ in their relationship to their information: A reporter has no personal relationship to the facts he is working with; a witness must have personal experience with them. The reporter knows nothing firsthand, but no witness is called to the stand unless he has personal involvement with the information (He saw the accident; he knows

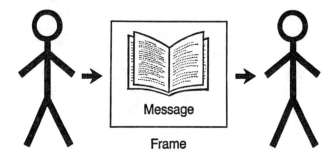

Figure 2. The frame is the vehicle which carries the data.

Communicative Method in Music Evangelism 49

the defendant or plaintiff, and so forth.). The Christian has experienced the new birth; he or she knows the Savior, and this will inevitably be an important inference in the mind of the receptor. It is a part of the message. Therefore the message is seen to be code plus frame plus initiator.

If we are witnesses, who we are and what our relationship is to our Information is an important part of the process for two very important reasons. One is that we are not alone in our communication; the Holy Spirit is active in us and in our receptors. A second reason is that our relationship to the data is itself a kind of information.

Much of what we want to relay must be *de*noted, that is, we are conveying *denotative* information, data which is objectively true without reference to the initator or receptor. Denotative information is limited, specific, and exact. If I say, "My neighbor has three children," your interpretation of my remark has no leeway regarding certain aspects of the information I have furnished you. The information is external to my reaction to it; it is limited (you know about where he lives if you know where I live), and it is specific (not two or four children).

But human communication is not limited to the objective, the limited, and the specific. We are always *con*noting our own relationship or reaction to objective fact. If I say, "That buzzard has a gillion kids," you know a great deal more about me than you do about the buzzard. You may not know whom I am talking about, or where he lives; you do not know how many children he has. But you do know that *I* think he lives too near me, that he has more children than I wish he had, and that they bother me. Connotative information is made up of data which is subjective in nature, and interprets an attitude or frame of reference of the initiator. It is suggestive and seeks, by implication, to impart information which is also essential and significant.

Therefore initiators have enormous responsibilities as they prepare to share a message. In communication, this preparation is called *encoding.* For the Christian witness, encoding is the choosing or creation of

50   Music in Missions: Discipling Through Music

a frame appropriate to the receptor's points of reference and the selection of appropriate data concerning sin, the person of Christ, and redemption on the basis of a receptor's present readiness. Seen in this light, encoding the gospel is a work of grace.

Frame

Initiators are under biblical constrain to adjust their frame to the receptor's informational (conceptual) modes (1 Cor. 9:19-22). For the trained musician, this may be difficult, for few prejudices are as strong as musical ones. Yet, since God is not limited to any human conceptual framework—"high" or "low," European or indigenous, rural or popular—and since the missionary call places the missionary musician under the same illustrious yoke as it did the apostle Paul, the reception of the message is more important than its transmission. For a music evangelist, the art lies not in the music itself but in the effective encoding of the message, in the choice of appropriate data in an effective sequence and in those delicate adjustments of the frame which will capture the attention, inclinations, and predilections of the receptor.

Just as radio waves may be jammed by anyone hostile to their reception, the informational target may react against the frame or even the data. He or she will send out negative waves countering an attempted transmission. This nullifying tide takes the form of a communication barrier. A barrier is a mental, spiritual, or psychological obstacle to the reception of information. Usually this term applies to aspects of the frame which a receptor finds objectionable although in some cases one may have a preexistent bias against the data itself (for example, against the divinity of Christ). If the objection is to the frame, we may easily change the frame. If the barrier is against the data, we do not change the data. We may, however, emphasize other nonobjectionable information *initially*, but only with the intent of presenting all necessary data after it has been prepared for.

Barriers erected this way shut out not only information but the intent and love of the initiator. In the occidental tradition, many church musicians establish their priorities within the confines of musical style alone. This is to assume a spiritual stance at variance with the biblical one (Phil. 2:3-8). My personal, customary frame of "art" music may be annoying or even painful to a hillbilly—or to almost anyone in the many streams of popular and commercial music, that is, to anyone outside my tradition.

On the other hand, if I adjust the frame to the receptor's mentality and world view, then the music is not a block to the information I am attempting to convey. The person becomes in fact a receptor rather than a mere target. Paul's concern for Philemon was that "the fellowship of your faith may become effective" (Philem. 6, NASB). The accomplishment of such effective sharing will require nothing less than a divine humility on the part of the initiator, and may be a considerably more splendid achievement than mere musical success. Perhaps in eternity the accomplishments of evangelistic musicians will be one of the astonishing achievements of art history. Furthermore, if the receptor responds by faith in Christ, he in turn will become an initiator, communicating to his own compatriots in that frame which is natural both to him and to them.

An important factor in securing attention and maintaining it is a proper use of signals. A *signal* is any agent which attracts attention.

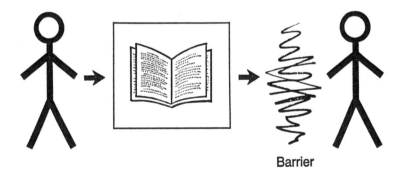

Figure 3. A negative reaction erects a barrier.

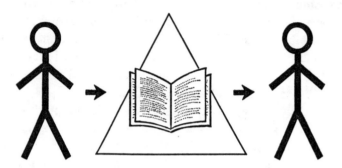

Figure 4. Changing the frame invites reception and renders retransmission possible

It may be a barking dog or an automobile horn. A signal will not function unless it affects one or more of the five senses in some way. The New Testament uses all five senses: for vision, the cross; for hearing, teaching and preaching; for touch, the holy kiss (Christ often touched those He was healing.); for taste and smell, the Lord's Supper.

The basic factor in signals is change. It may be a change of senses—from communicating through sight to communicating through sound, for example, from a picture to a song. It may be a change in sense factor—in sight, a change of color; in sound, a change of volume, and so forth. In music, signals function in any pronounced musical change: a high note, a high volume, or a low volume if it has been on some other level, a change of key or rhythm, and so forth.

Code

The most significant information our target will need, however, will be the denotative data. A certain corpus of objective truth must be intelligently apprehended if the receptor is to take a meaningful step toward Jesus Christ. Although the initiator may have chosen the frame very carefully, he or she still has the task of selecting which data are essential for authentic conversion. We may need to convince

Communicative Method in Music Evangelism 53

some people of the divinity of of Jesus. If that knowledge is lacking or incompletely understood, keeping Him before the eyes of our target is not a waste of time. Some cultures lack a developed concept of sin; their concept of wrong is action (not attitude) against society or people, leading to shame, and yet sin is against God. Where that concept is absent, we must help our prospects in their understanding of the holy nature of God and the seriousness of offense against Him. It will always be wise to choose our data with the needs of the target audience in mind. In other words, the data must be appropriate to their current frame of reference.[2]

We must not inundate the receptor with too much information at once, especially if he or she has little background to understand the Christian message. Effective evangelists compile their tracts with the idea of presenting a few essential ideas: *four* spiritual laws, *five* steps to peace with God, and so forth. Sermons are limited in their number of essential points. Generally, communication theory now tends to emphasize that the mind cannot accept very much new information at one time, but it is evident that God did not wait on the twentieth century to develop His method. Two thousand years ago Paul declared, "I determined not to know any thing among you, save Jesus Christ, and him crucified" (1 Cor. 2:2). Time will not bring new techniques but a sharpening and refining of what He has provided from the beginning.

We are now ready to proceed to the synthesizing of method in musical evangelism. We have seen the importance of the frame chosen, the care we must take in selecting data appropriate to the target's frame of reference, and the limitation we must place on the amount of data. In our case, the frame is musical. We have many effective patterns of effective data (at least for most areas in the West) in the form of small tracts. Perhaps the best known of these is *The Four Spiritual Laws*, published by Campus Crusade. If we were to state these laws in sequence orally, add a Scripture to each one, sing a hymn (or any kind of song) with each of the laws to heighten the connotative value of its effect, we would have a presentation that followed all the

54   Music in Missions: Discipling Through Music

principles outlined above. The appendix demonstrates just such a presentation.

The addition of the Scripture is important. "So shall my word be that goeth forth out of my mouth: it shall not return unto me void, but it shall accomplish that which I please, and it shall prosper in the thing whereto I sent it" (Isa. 55:11). If we are faithful to the spirit of Scripture, we add a supernatural plus to the work.

Since we need a vocabulary to facilitate our work, let us call this combination of Scripture, song, and message a code stucture. A *code structure* is a group of data chosen to introduce the Person of Jesus Christ and His salvation, arranged in an order that will be meaningful and comprehensive on the basis of the receptor's present base of information, and stated or placed in a frame suitable to communicate both denotative and connotative information appropriate to the receptor's life orientation.

This procedure is distinctive in the strong emphasis it places on the receptors and their reactions. We must exert ourselves as strongly as possible to think as they think, to anticipate their reactions. Does this mean we are seeking to be crowd pleasers? If that were true, the music alone would be our primary preoccupation. However, our central and primary objective is the effective transmission of information. We categorically reject any music which in style or text contradicts, conflicts with, or violates the divine style of the Person of Christ. We would reject any music which contradicted that aspect of the message we were currently working with.

It severely limits the quantity of information. The evangelist has two great concerns: a message which cannot be compromised and a person who must be reached with that message. Ultimately, persons must understand the demands of Christ and how to know Him— they must know the plan of salvation. But reaching them may take time, especially if their informational base is small. In that case, the initial efforts might focus on a single aspect of Christ's personality or being (love, joy, peace) or the central Christian doctrines about His work in salvation (reconciliation, atonement, and so forth.). It might

Communicative Method in Music Evangelism 55

center on some major datum (Christ's role in creation) of significance in the receptor's environment or culture.

If the receptor's base of information is large, the data may be more inclusive (the four spiritual laws). If the receptor's information contains erroneous data, the structure should focus on the particular corrective needed (in predominantly Roman Catholic countries, the accessibility of Christ as a Person or personal faith in Him; in Moslem areas, a special emphasis on Christ's divinity or on the unity of the Godhead). Although we may expect certain other data such as human sinfulness to be conveyed by the Holy Spirit when a real confrontation with Christ is effected, this information should more often than not be explicitly stated and clarified.

The appendix contains a code structure built on the twenty-third Psalm with the various verses relating the Shepherd Lord to Christ. The "valley of the shadow of death" (v. 4) becomes an opportunity to refer to the Lord's death on the cross. The points are heightened with various musical settings. The use of signal can be seen in the many changes: changes of direction (by placing speakers in different parts of the auditorium) and changes of musical setting (from choral to congregational singing). Even the use of a familiar hymn tune ("Joyful Song") and text (from "Praise Him! Praise Him!") with the harmony radically altered will serve as a signal for those familiar with the hymn.

The short musical settings are offered also as an example of a technique which will be effective in music evangelism. They are composed in the style advocated by Hindemith with his *Gebrauchsmusik,* that is, *music for use.* Hindemith's idea was to return music to the simplicity of earlier times when the average layperson could perform almost any music of the day. Since the term is already in use, the idea should be ideal for the purposes of music evangelism. In our context here, *Gebrauchsmusik* is a brief musical statement, long enough to state or reinforce a single idea, deliberately curtailed by avoiding musical development or argument so as not to detract from the central idea(s). *Gebrauchsmusik* need not be the resetting of a hymn, as here

56 Music in Missions: Discipling Through Music

but could even consist of brief direct statements from hymns as they are found in the hymnal.

No one format is the correct format. Other examples in the appendix demonstrate the wide variety of approaches possible. The frame could be a congregational worship service, choir or choral programs, sacred concerts, cantatas, dramas, multimedia, chalk talks, flannelgraph presentations, and so forth. An almost endless variety of structures are available: tracts, psalms or other Bible passages, hymns (see "Christ the Word of God" in appendix 1, topical or thematic programs, narration of a story, and so forth).

Principles in Selecting a Frame

1. *The initiator's primary concern is the mental and conceptual framework of the receptor.* The initiator assumes a servant attitude. "For though I be free from all men, yet have I made myself servant unto all, that I might gain the more" (1 Cor. 9:19).

2. *Initial impressions constitute a signal which must capture the receptor.* They should be either pleasant or intriguing. "Walk in wisdom toward them that are without, redeeming the time. Let your speech be alway with grace, seasoned with salt" (Col. 4:5-6).

3. *Comprehensibility and intelligibility are basic requisites for the frame.*

4. *The frame must be meaningful in terms of the receptor's personality.* Connotative meanings are conveyed by the frame. The musical language should be as close as possible to the receptor's "first" musical language.

> Unto the Jews I became as a Jew, that I might gain the Jews; to them that are under the law, as under the law, that I might gain them that are under the law; . . . To the weak became I as weak, that I might gain the weak: I am made all things to all men, that I might by all means save some (1 Cor. 9:20-23).

5. *The frame must maintain attention.* Some attention getters are: something unusual (mildly, not shockingly, different) and something pleasant. Some attention losers are: sameness (continuation of one

Communicative Method in Music Evangelism 57

thing too long) and irrelevance (no meaning for the receptor's life). Some attention maintainers are: changes (any kind—changes in volume; change of speakers, especially male to female; changes in the number of speakers; changes of medium, and so forth.) and skillful use of the visual. The visual usually provides more opportunity for maintaining attention than the other senses. Attention can be visually shifted to various parts of the stage or pulpit; other visual changes include movement, changes of color. The occasional introduction of various sound effects acts as a signal: bells, drums, solo instruments, footsteps, and so forth. Music can be varied by shifts from a cappella to accompanied music, changes of tempo, key, style, or singing voices. Instrumental music is generally best for "mood" music, sections without narration.

Principles in Building a Code Structure

1. *Pare to the minimum.* Usually four to six major points are enough; you may need fewer if your area is less literate.

2. *Data should be articulated as specifically as you can.* Each point should in some way direct the receptor toward an encounter with Christ and salvation.

3. *Prayerfully depend on God's direction.* This (and the next two points) take advantage of the supernatural plus. "Which things also we speak, not in the words which man's wisdom teacheth, but which the Holy Ghost teacheth" (1 Cor. 2:13).

4. *Use Scripture.*

5. *Jesus Christ is the central theme of every code.* Various aspects may be emphasized, but the gospel requires the centrality of Christ.

Methodology

Two general types of music evangelism may be employed, depending on the circumstances: inducement evangelism and direct evangelism.[3] *Inducement evangelism* is that which does not demand a confrontation with decision but is intended to provide the receptor with preliminary information that will prepare him or her for a valid choice. It belongs to the early stages of our strategy and is useful where there is time to lay groundwork for confrontation with Christ. Its purpose is frankly evangelistic, but we must face the fact that in some cases our targets may need far more knowledge than their backgrounds provide. In inducement evangelism we are seeking to win a hearing for the gospel.

Direct evangelism is that which aims to present a crisis of decision in which the receptor, under the leadership of the Holy Spirit, faces the reality of life with or without Christ. The communicative process is telescoped in this type of evangelism. It is assumed that when a crisis of choosing is precipitated, we will be fairly certain that the receptors are fully aware, and probably convinced, of the nature of sin, the divinity of Christ, and the validity of His offer because of His work on the cross.

There are two methods of presenting Christ through music: ambulatory evangelism and feature evangelism. *Ambulatory evangelism* or encounter evangelism occurs when we attempt to present any kind of musical program in an impromptu situation. This kind of evangelism has the advantage that it catches many who would not go to a concert hall or church. Its disadvantage is that it is dependent on chance for its prospects. Missionary Antonio (Tony) Anaya had an effective outreach through brief programs with guitar which he would present on the beach in Spain in the early 1970s. These also might be presented in parks or in other public places. It is important to check to see if such presentations are legal and to obtain permission if the presentation is on commercial property.

Feature evangelism is the presentation of a planned musical program for evangelistic purposes in the formal setting of an auditorium, hotel lobby, convention center, or other public building. Its principal advantage is that the audience brings to the program a certain readiness. Their presence itself indicates some interest in the presentation, if not in its purpose. Its disadvantage is that it is more expensive and requires considerable logistical preparation.

History is replete with stories of men and women who found

Communicative Method in Music Evangelism

Christ through a musical presentation of some kind. Musicians have been gifted with one of the most powerful tools in creation for bringing others to Christ. In eternity, many will confess that they owe their spiritual life to the expense or trouble that dedicated music evangelists went to in order to provide the opportunity which God used for purposes grander than we can imagine.

Notes

1. See Marshall McLuhan and Quentin Fiore, *The Medium Is the Massage* [sic] (New York: Bantam Books, 1967), *passim;* and McLuhan, *Understanding Media* (New York: McGraw-Hill, 1964), pp. 7-21.

2. The author once knew a Pakistani Christian who was raised a strict Moslem. He stated that through the first part of his life he was repulsed by Christians who tried to convince him of the Trinity. What finally brought him to Christ was a godly teacher who simply exalted Christ without argument. Slowly coming to perceive the real nature of Christ's person, he perceived His divinity, and accepted Him. The earlier Christians had chosen true but not-yet-appropriate data in their efforts to win him.

3. The gist of these classifications was originally presented by the author in "Music in World Evangelism," *The Commission,* Apr. 1971, pp. 24-26.

4

Principles of Training

Institutional Music Teaching

The difference in institutional mission teaching and teaching in a mission church is only a matter of degree. In missions situations, very little music training is of music specialists. In the churches, we are helping members learn to exercise the gift of music; in the institutions, we are usually training the pastors who will teach the members. Most countries with a longer history of mission activity also have regional and national workshops of various kinds. The general principles will be the same but will differ somewhat in the degree of attainment we expect of the students. This chapter, therefore, will concentrate on the training of leaders—mainly the pastors, with other workers also at times. The principles will apply anywhere.

A variety of names designate institutions assigned the responsibility of preparing adult Christian leaders for the work of the ministry. The very presence of such an institution usually indicates that mission advance has a secure foothold and that trained workers are in some demand in a given country. Generally the name "seminary" or "theological college" (as distinct from "Bible college") carries approximately the same meaning that it carries in the United States, that is, an institution for graduate training beyond the university. "Theological institutes" or "Bible institutes" (and in some cases, "Bible college"), on the other hand, are usually a provision for those called into Christian service who have a less formal educational back-

Principles of Training 61

ground. "International seminaries" are sometimes provided for a group of countries, often with a common language (Spanish in South America), or where a trade language is common to a community of nations (English in Europe).[1]

As in North America, the same institution often provides training for those eligible for seminary and for those whose background require an institute. However, there exists a wide disparity between entrance requirements at seminaries and between the actual products of seminaries and institutes. It is quite possible that in some cases, a diploma from an institute indicates more thorough training than some seminary degrees. The same cadre of teachers and the same institutional resources may be used in either case; the basic commission from a given church body to educate the ministry is equally binding on both. For the present, the same general methodology and educational principles will apply to either, with adjustments made with reference to the local situation. Whether seminary or institute, the greatest single variant will be the musical background of the students, and adjustment to this factor must permeate all thinking and planning of administrators and faculty.

Before we can ask, "What shall we teach?" (curriculum), we must ask *whom* we are teaching. Only a fraction of overseas seminaries offer degrees in music.[2] Therefore music teachers in seminaries and institutes on most mission fields are basically concerned with providing training for pastors who must administer the entire church program, other workers preparing for multiple responsibilities, and some laypersons. We rarely teach (for example) career performers. Because of this, the missionary seminary teacher labors under a mandate considerably more difficult and lofty than appears on the surface. Technical training is, after all, limited, and therefore easier.

Curriculum will also grow out of the stated purposes of an institution. The missionary teacher teaching in an institution will do well to study the statement of purpose, usually found in the institution's catalog. Along with the general purposes of ministry, different institutions state various other emphases in their catalog. Some empha-

62   **Music in Missions: Discipling Through Music**

size extension of the kingdom of God (International Baptist Theological Seminary, Colombia; The Malaysia Baptist Theological Seminary; etc.); some emphasize development of permanent devotional habits (The Taiwan Baptist Seminary); some require a degree of specialization in a major field (Asia Baptist Graduate Theological Seminary, Hong Kong); and so forth. Virtually all state, in one form or another, that their main purpose is to train leaders for ministry in churches. These are institutional (not departmental) purposes, and it would be a helpful exercise for instructors consciously to articulate ways in which they could discover application of them in the courses they teach.

Education is essentially (1) the alteration of behavior and (2) making articulate those conceptual processes of a given discipline which facilitate the alteration of behavior. Growing itself brings an alteration of behavior. What do we want to alter? Musically, the alteration desired is the improvement of a rather large number of skills. The most important of these skills are performance and the ability to hear and respond to music. Two kinds of training are employed to facilitate the improvement of skill areas: private or class lessons in a performance area and classes in which hearing and response patterns are drilled on (theory, sightsinging, ear training, written work in harmony and counterpoint, analysis, and so forth). This kind of theoretical training is normally taken earlier in a course of study than training in music ministry, presumably to allow time for maturation of the skills.

The various overseas schools report that usually some musical skill and understanding is expected of all students at the end of their training.[3] It seems to be a rare case in which a school does not require some music of all students. Courses most frequently required are conducting, piano, and theory; other requirements are "general music" (usually with rudiments of music being the major part), choir, ministry of music, hymnology, and music appreciation. These courses are often combined in various ways. Some institutions require piano of all women (for example, International Baptist Theo-

Principles of Training 63

logical Seminary in Colombia), a highly practical requirement in view of the shortage of accompanists in most fields. The average number of music courses required of theological students is about three. This exceeds the average number required in North American seminaries, but in most overseas churches the pastor has to shoulder the entire burden of all musical activity in the church more frequently than in North America. It is appropriate to continue these requirements.

Those who offer music degrees tend to specialize somewhat less than their North American counterparts, that is, the degree plans at least offer less specialization. There does not seem to be a typical degree plan; specific requirements should vary from one seminary to another because of varying stages of development and because of varying local cultures. It is safe to generalize that the degree plans approximate those of Europe and North America with less emphasis on performance.

On the music degree plans, theory credits offered include theory, sightsinging, harmony, counterpoint, form, analysis (or a combination of form and analysis), composition (or composition and arranging), and conducting. Named among history courses are music appreciation, art history, music history, national music, and choral literature. The ministry of music courses include such courses as music in worship, hymnology, ministry of music (presumably general techniques with emphasis on the program of the church, that is, church music administration), "Bible music," and choral techniques.[4] Recently, new courses were being introduced such as church music education. Performance areas include piano, organ, harmonium, hymn playing, voice, vocal pedagogy, recorder, trumpet, recital (usually given in the last year of study), guitar, and choir. Usually absent are orchestration, musicology, keyboard literature, organ familiarization, liturgies, psychology of church music, vocal diction, and score reading.

Physical Factors

Enrollment

The purpose of a seminary or institute is to train national leaders; enrollment in the schools should keep pace with the growth of the churches, both to supply workers for new churches and to replace losses. In rapidly expanding areas, the number of churches often exceeds the number of available national pastors. Where the ratio tends to establish a balance, it is possible that spiritual advance has become quiescent. If church growth is assumed to be the criterion for mission advance, the ideal will not be reached until seminary or institute enrollments march apace with conversions; the ideal here is considered to be national pastors and workers for national churches.[5]

Adequate recruitment will be a product of (1) a spirit of indigenization, (2) spiritual advance, and (3) informing potential students about the institution. The best instrument for disseminating information is a printed institutional catalog; most overseas schools now have catalogs although they are not always reprinted at regular intervals. Music teachers and departments might additionally prepare a brochure on the available offerings in music. Choir tours provide an opportunity to draw attention to the school; printed material (catalogs, brochures, programs) in the hands of the audiences provide a permanent reminder for those interested. Some schools report that the primary purpose of choir tours is promotion of the institution; others stated that tours were both evangelistic and promotional.

Equipment

It is an ancient truism that the quality of education depends primarily on the faculty, is strongly conditioned by the library, and helped only incidentally by buildings and equipment. Interestingly, complaints from missionary musicians about the physical properties of schools are seldom heard. Nevertheless, good equipment does facilitate experience (whereby we learn) and moreover is a source of

Principles of Training 65

(perhaps subconscious) encouragement to faculty and students. All seminaries supported in part by the Southern Baptist Foreign Mission Board and offering music degrees have several pianos. A majority of the seminaries and most of the institutes have studios and practice areas. Classrooms are often shared with other courses, although in a few cases the institution has music classrooms or even a music building (for example, the Baptist seminaries in Cali, Recife, and Rio de Janeiro). Recording equipment is often borrowed from or shared with radio technicians, where this ministry is also available. Duplication processes are widely available, usually mimeograph, but also some carbon-transfer processes.

Teaching aids are frequently available, especially in urban areas. Two expediencies may facilitate teaching where such equipment is unavailable: improvisation and the use of furlough to purchase supplies. Many items can be improvised on the field: flash cards, note spellers, and even dummy keyboards. Heavy black ink should be used, and precautions to make them permanent will save time later. Early in each term, missionary musicians should begin making a list of unavailable items which they truly believe they need so that they can purchase them on furlough. To facilitate written work, one might also check with a good secretary soon after coming on furlough to get items new on the market that speed up writing processes. Many items commercially marketed in the United States can be obtained in other forms elsewhere; carbon tetrachloride is an excellent and cheaper substitute for American type cleaners.

The library has no substitute. Most institutions report extremely inadequate library holdings. A varied selection of music books in the national language is rarely available except in more advanced cultures such as Spanish-, Portuguese-, Chinese-, or Japanese-speaking areas. The lacunae in church music books remains painful everywhere.[6] Scores (anthems and sheet music) are found only in those rare countries with a longer history of music in the institutions. Even there usable choral music in the national language is in short supply. Discs and tapes are becoming more available, but these are often

Music in Missions: Discipling Through Music

locally produced and are not commercially available. One missionary reports the clever solution of using tapes from the radio studio for teaching purposes.

Excellent theory texts are available in all European languages and in the high cultures of the Orient. These often follow the curriculum established by the national conservatory requirements (which may seem in some cases to violate educational principles), but perhaps in the final analysis the local curriculum will best serve the purposes of national musicians who, after all, must remain in dialogue with their compatriots. If a given curriculum seems to move too rapidly or to divorce musical vocabulary from musical experience, an adaptation of the system may be used. Conservatory texts without modification are often not appropriate to the level required in mission areas. Obviously weekend clinics in rural churches should not attempt the conservatory approach. The only satisfactory solution to the problem of materials for clinics in rural areas is self-prepared syllabi. I have examined several of these from various areas, and they often are quite successful.

The very small quantity of books available on ministry of music, hymnology, and so forth, pose one of the most serious challenges to music missions. Institutions worldwide report holdings in English, sometimes extensive. From the standpoint of mission methodology, it is unfortunate that often no or few resources are available in the local languages, and yet in the context of a higher institution it would be unrealistic to negate the value of these English sources, at least for research. It is equally ill-advised to force national patterns into an American or European mold (see chapter 7). The only solution at this point lies in the skill of the missionary who can adapt a concept or program so skillfully to the national pattern that nationals will not be aware of its origin. Some principles are universal, and where they are not the missionary must be sensitive.

It appears likely that for years yet the English-speaking world will furnish valuable resources in church music; for the present, we must make do with what we have. Nevertheless it would behoove music

Principles of Training 67

missionaries to encourage the writing of textbooks and to translate those whose information can be transferred without damage to indigenous progress (such as Paul McCommon's *Music in the Bible*).

Faculty

The general rule seems to be part-time faculty for institutes (with several notable exceptions) and a combination of full-time and part-time teachers for the colleges and seminaries. The seminaries with degree programs make excellent use of national teachers while smaller schools often use only missionary teachers. This seems to be a natural pattern. To some extent, so long as a majority of the churches in a given country are not self-supporting, missionaries will remain a useful resource for music teaching. Missionaries are graduates of institutions that have profited from long experience with training Christian workers.

But it must also be remembered that missionaries bring to institutional teaching the same problems that they bring to other missionary activities: they work in a second language, and local cultural thought patterns are different, even antithetical, at times to that of the missionary. Missionaries at times become outstanding teachers, but the very role of missionary is that of catalyst. They may be well integrated into the *koinonia* of their national fellowship, but they do themselves a disservice if they situate themselves in a permanent teaching position and abandon the incisive thrust of encouraging national leaders. Effective missions has always carried a pioneering spirit into new areas.

For effective institutional ministry, the basic staff of a school as it grows should remain in a process of becoming increasingly national. Nationals make immediate and idiomatic contact with the specific learning problems and opportunities their students offer them. The best music missionary teachers are constantly on the lookout for national teachers as the ministry of the institution broadens.

Principles

Worthy course planning will ask the following questions: (1) In what ways does this course serve the defined purposes of the institution? (2) Which specific behavior must be altered in this area for more effective Christian service? From this question will emanate the approach to a given class. (3) Which concepts need clarifying and articulating for adequate understanding of the material? Exploration of the latter question will lead to a formulation (or selection) of appropriate vocabulary, or to the adoption of existent terminology, and a means of clarifying it.

Theory

Theory itself is neither sacred nor secular; it may be profaned or sanctified by the use to which it is put. In the light of question (1) above, the essential purpose of theory is to enable Christians to sing praises more effectively, that is, not more "correctly" but more easily, and so hopefully to free the heart. It will be a lovely day when teachers enter theory classes with the delighted enthusiasm of an infectious singing heart. Technical mastery does render singing more intelligent (Correctness is a smaller part of intelligent performance.) and intelligence, being under the control of the will, may indeed be joyfully placed at the service of heart song.

Questions (2) and (3) are more closely bound together in music theory than other aspects of music training, for the understanding of tonal relationships grows as grasp of the vocabulary becomes meaningful. Students should be introduced to the scale, not by memory or rote methods, but by demonstration of what a scale is, that is, the tonal materials of a given music.

The method given here is to teach *the conceptual process in which music is heard;* this procedure has been used many times in mission situations.[7] It is very effective, for example, to list all the notes used by a composer in a given melody, say the first line of "Sweet Hour." All the notes used throughout the hymn are found in the first line, given

Principles of Training

here in order of appearance and without repeating any note:

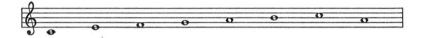

Figure 1. Notes used in "Sweet Hour."

The same series, arranged in order of ascending pitches, is nothing more than a systematic *list*:

Figure 2. Notes in "Sweet Hour" arranged as a "list."

Obviously "Sweet Hour" was chosen because it gives us a hymn in which all the notes are contained within the tonic octave, but this need not be noted at this point. It is not yet necessary that the student understand the relationship of range to tonic; he or she must first know that a scale is simply a *list* (and it should be noted in teaching that the list is here numbered). Then we may proceed to an understanding of function.

Reasons for differences in terminology will help the missionary music teacher communicate function more efficiently. In all world areas where Western music has gained a secure foothold (which includes virtually all urban areas outside the Communist bloc), the

70   Music in Missions: Discipling Through Music

missionary must be aware of differences in conceptual processes between the local world view as expressed in music and in the imported Western product. In the European-American complex descended from Rameau's theories and Germanic functional harmony, one must be especially aware of the underlying quality in most Western music of alternating tension with relaxation of tension.

Western music centers around a rest tone, the tonic, the note on which a piece of music often comes to rest—the final relaxation of tension in a piece of music. In diatonic music, the tonic is the first note or degree of the scale. This tendency of music to gravitate toward the tonic (or somewhere in the chord based on the tonic) is called *tonicity*. It is effective in teaching this concept to demonstrate the tendency of Western acculturated ears to tonicity by playing a progression that does not end in tonic and then contrasting it with one that does. If your students are sensitive to tonality, you may even run a glissando on the white notes and ask the class to hum the tonal "center of gravity" (C Natural or Do) that floats to their consciousness; follow this with a glissando on the black notes, which normally produces a feeling that F Sharp is tonic.

After explaining this tendency, for contrast introduce the meaning of the "leading tone," or seventh degree of the scale, although the students need not yet be aware of what a scale is, as such. These concepts are simply explained as notes they need be familiar with. In explaining it, special emphasis should be placed on the tension the leading tone produces; the name for the leading tone in the Romance languages is "sensitive note" (for example, Spanish "nota sensible").[8] It is also helpful to note the close proximity of the leading tone to the tonic, striking the two together to dramatize the magnitude of their dissonance; it is a tense combination. Had the seventh note been a whole step lower than the tonic (rather than a half step), it would have shown less tension, been less dissonant.

The fifth degree, the dominant, should be explained by stating that the very name describes what this degree does: it dominates. This is true throughout the world in most musical systems; the fifth (mea-

Principles of Training

suring by our scale) has a dominating tendency in some way. It is possible that the natural tendency of the ear to select a perfect fifth as the basic consonance of the scale, after the octave, is due to the natural phenomenon of the strength of the fifth in the harmonic (or overtone) series. The subdominant, then, is literally an "underdominant," and its name does not mean that it is under the dominant; it is an under-*fifth*, a fifth below tonic. Rameau diagrammed it:

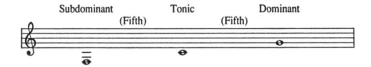

Figure 3. The two dominants, a fifth below and above tonic.

For students, it will probably be more useful to return to the original "list," and mark the two dominants as being a fifth *above* the lower tonic, and a fifth *below* the upper tonic.

Figure 4. The dominants relating to upper and lower tonic.

Therefore we have four "Functional Names"—tonic, leading tone, dominant, and subdominant—whose names describe their *function* within the scale.

72   Music in Missions: Discipling Through Music

The other notes of the scale, by contrast, are "Positional Names" whose names explain their position in the scale. The second degree, "supertonic," is literally (as in Latin) *above* the tonic. Since the basic and controlling consonance of the scale consists of the tonic and dominant, the midpoint between them is called "mediant"—middle.

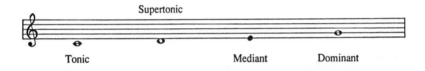

Figure 4. Positional degrees of the scale.

The midpoint between the upper tonic and *sub*dominant, in English, is *sub*mediant.

Figure 5. Submediant related to the subdominant and tonic

Positional names, then, describe geography while functional

Principles of Training 73

names describe what a note tends to do. It is useful at this point in teaching the diatonic system to demonstrate functional harmony, especially with a series of secondary dominants, to dramatize the building and release of tension. Oriental music, by contrast, tends to be not dynamic but coloristic; each sound is valued for its own color or characteristic.

However, here we encounter a language difficulty: in Spanish and Portuguese, the sixth degree name does not describe its position between tonic and subdominant, but rather its position above the dominant; it is "superdominant." It is possible that history can account for this: in fugal procedure, within the fugue subject, if the supertonic degree was used in a characteristic way to relate it to the tonic as the note above it, it was answered by the second of dominant (which was how fugal writers described it). Other contexts demanded that the third above dominant be treated as an uncharacteristic melody note (instead of a chordal implication), so that it could be answered by the supertonic. The entire problem was posed by the short distance between dominant and upper tonic as contrasted with the greater distance between lower tonic and dominant. Very complex but specific rules governed the answering of tonic by dominant and vice versa.

It will be unnecessary to point out to students that the sixth degree is named differently in European languages or to conjecture on reasons for the difference. (Few are literate enough to know fugal procedure, and the wisdom of attempting to bring it in is highly questionable!). What is important for the missionary is to accept the differing terminology as valid and to provide students with meaning for their musical experience. In either case, the sixth degree is positional.

This will be significant when students begin to encounter minor scales. Between parallel major and minor functional degrees are invariable—they will be the same notes in the two modes—while positional degrees may be altered:

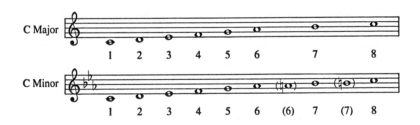

Figure 6. Major and minor variable positional degrees

This rule still holds true for the seventh degree, for a true leading tone will always be a half step below tonic; a whole step does not generate the necessary tension. The lowered seventh is not correctly a leading tone, but a *subtonic*, which is a positional name not a functional one.[9]

From this point of departure—an understanding of *function*—students may be led to hear alternating tension and relaxation, may be more specific about sound and its effects, and (with experience and keyboard practice) may even be led into more accurate sightsinging and dictation. The hearing behavior will have been altered by an understanding of the concepts, which in turn will also be clearer and more articulate.

Conducting

The purpose of conducting is that congregations sing well, sing together, and that the unity of their singing might express the unity

Principles of Training

of their spirit. The second and third questions above (under "Principles") will be answered if (1) we teach rhythm accurately and effectively, and (2) we communicate our intentions to choir and congregation well.

Rhythm is the most difficult of all musical phenomena to teach. As with all learning, a good teacher proceeds from experience to articulation of that experience with proper vocabulary. The order of presentation probably should be: (1) beat, (2) meter, (3) patterns organized in and around the beats, and (4) tempo.

Beat should first be experienced in a well-known hymn or song and students led to describe the phenomenon in nontechnical terms. Two explanations should be helpful: beat occurs regularly (spaced evenly apart) and may be compared to other aural and visual phenomena. (Draw a picture of evenly spaced marks to represent beat.) Meter can be introduced by leading students to discover without technical vocabulary the periodic recurrence of strong beats. The fact that strong beats occur in well-known hymns in series of two, three, and four will be a basis for the introduction of the concept of the measure. Patterns might be taught (for example) by placing visual patterns against a scrim representing beats evenly spaced. As students perceive that some notes last across several beats while others move more rapidly than the beat itself, it is natural to lead them into a study of note values and relationships.[10] Good rhythmic reading, however, is best produced by a great deal of experience in combining rhythmic patterns. For example, the Hazel Cobb piano method, in which one memorizes a given pattern and reproduces it in a number of contexts, has great promise for the imaginative teacher.

The communication of rhythm (conducting) has as its purpose the unifying of group singing. Once this basic fact is acknowledged and is meaningful to the student, technical procedures may follow. The gestures given in various texts are suggestive and are only a beginning. A good conductor will lead the choir and congregation into sensitivity to much more than mere gesture. Much is communicated

76   Music in Missions: Discipling Through Music

by body movement and attitude, by inflections and size of the gestures, by the face, and especially by the spirit.

Ministry of Music

Why include ministry of music at all in mission institutions? Because, ultimately, we hope to facilitate the functioning of the church in worship and in evangelism. The purpose of hymnology is to enable a congregation to sing with spirit and intelligence. Concepts will need to be clarified: What is a hymn? Why did the author use this and not that imagery? How does meter affect the mood of the poem? What linguistic effects please the ear as music does? How does this theology relate to my life?

The purpose of music administration is to channel musical activity into productive activity. Teachers of administration activities are basically concerned with how people learn: How can we enable the child to release rhythmic energy? What purpose will this music serve among the young people? How can we work with choirs so that they will grow and communicate God more effectively to the congregation?

Blessed would be the students who were taught to make their own list of questions growing out of the three listed above under "Principles." Inevitably, the questions would differ from church to church, and from school to school.

Choir

Institutional choirs have been among the most effective of all mission efforts. They encounter a full gamut of problems: too many male voices with consequent choral imbalance, lack of instruments and sometimes facilities on tour, inadequate supply of literature, and so forth. Still, probably no other institutional activity has produced so high a yield as choirs. They encourage the churches, they often net converts in their evangelistic services, they advertise the cause of Christ, and they bring students to the schools.

The problem of instruments has occasionally been solved by pre-

Principles of Training 77

paring music that could use portable instruments—especially guitar and accordion. Problems of balance are sometimes met by the organization of several smaller ensembles. The choral sound is a natural communicator of Christian unity and of musical beauty; response to it justifies its continuation in spite of the obstacles. In some areas, students have expressed gratitude for a shared opportunity to witness through choirs. It can also be a means of welding school spirit. Membership in the choir has been, under imaginative leaders, a badge of honor eagerly sought in some institutions.

Keyboard

Keyboard has the advantage of associating tonal relationships with a visual measure of space. Theory teachers regularly report that instrumentalists perform more accurately on sight-singing and dictation than noninstrumentalists. In addition, one of the most serious shortages in most countries is accompanists.

Keyboard teachers should especially be mindful of thorough grounding in theory—especially scales, arpeggios, and elementary keyboard harmony. Scale fingerings are built on the relationship of the shape of the hand to the keyboard (for example, in keys with five black notes, the longer fingers, two, three, and four, play the black notes, which are further from the body, and the thumbs or little fingers play the white notes), and much drill on scales seems to improve fingering in other pieces without conscious effort. All keyboard students should play hymns; they are an invaluable source for developing keyboard sense.

Both voice and keyboard may be taught in classes or privately. Occasionally organ or harmonium is also taught in classes. Classes on the mission field are usually quite small, and very nearly approach private instruction in the quality of time that can be given to each student.

To our principles should be added the importance of some kind of field work. Most schools make some provision for practical experience in weekend church work; some report the use of the chapel for

78   Music in Missions: Discipling Through Music

this purpose, and others report various additional kinds of church services as opportunities to give experience. A majority of institutions provide or assign some kind of summer activity.

The Future

Several countries have indicated needs for special thrusts in education. Developing countries often report a need for elementary theory classes available in the churches, because no music education is offered in public schools. Countries with an older history of evangelical Christianity report a need for workers able to combine music with a second or third specialized ministry. Countries such as Japan and Brazil now have a few full-time ministers of music in churches. Certainly a universal ideal will always be the recruitment and preparation of national teachers to train leaders.

These specific needs could well be met by reports of expanding extension work reported by many institutions. It appears very likely that seminaries and institutes around the world will need to give serious attention to techniques for making some level of leadership training available for larger masses of people. Nearly all schools report some kind of extension work now in progress, and ministry of music training would lend itself well to this kind of training. No doubt the North American format of training will need to be radically revised as various new approaches to theological education are developed.

Extension work will mean considerably more travel for most institutional music teachers. It will demand creativity in teaching methods where elaborate equipment cannot be transported easily. For some it will mean an adjustment in the musical level of work being taught now. It will entail some humility and some thought on musical styles that adequately express the heart song of rural areas. There will be some surprises that none can foresee now.

But that is our calling. Complacency is the disease of the unyielded. The missionary is a catalyst. Unimaginative people do not follow their God across another continent or to an unfamiliar part of their

Principles of Training 79

own country. Missionaries are a different breed—they *have* followed. Their very presence on the field indicates imagination. They are the called.

Brethren, I count not myself to have apprehended: but this one thing I do, forgetting those things which are behind, and reaching forth unto those things which are before, *I press toward the mark for the prize of the high calling of God in Christ Jesus* (Phil. 3:13-14, author's italics).

Notes

1. Examples are the International Baptist Theological Seminary in Cali, Colombia, which draws students from Central America, South America, and the Caribbean, and the Baptist Theological Seminary of Rüschlikon-Zürich, where a functional knowledge of English is an entrance requirement.

2. Among Baptists, only North and South American seminaries offer music degrees on a continuing basis. On other continents, training in music fundamentals is sometimes quite thorough in theological institutes, without leading to a music degree as such. This does not mean, however, that the seminary concerns itself exclusively with ministry; most overseas seminaries offer courses in music rudiments and very little in specialized music ministry.

3. In the fourteen years, 1967-1984, at least three questionnaires were taken, at Southwestern Baptist Theological Seminary in Fort Worth, Texas, of Southern Baptist missionaries concerning various aspects of their work. A general survey of other agencies mentioned in the foreword was also made. Most of the data in the section following were taken from these sources. Interviews with teachers in Africa reveal that theoretical training there is generally less inclusive. On the other hand, in some cases, missionary teachers in Africa have attempted to help nationals systematize and notate some of their indigenous music (Nathan Corbett in Kenya, Marilyn McMillan in Tanzania, Jerry Robertson in Ivory Coast and so forth). Many music missionaries in the Orient have pioneered in the use of ethnic music in Christian worship and in evangelism (Rennie Ohtani in Japan, Nita Jones in Korea, and so forth).

4. Choral Techniques may be classified either as a Ministry of Music course or a performance course, according to the emphasis of the instructor.

5. Sufficient deployment of the training-equipping ministry might also be accomplished by extension work. See "The Future," at the end of this chapter.

6. Japan has some excellent church-music handbooks; some books on hymnology and ministry of music (somewhat dated) are available in Spanish and Portuguese. Useful texts are available in the other European languages, but it is difficult to find these for sale in those African areas where a European language is the trade language.

80   Music in Missions: Discipling Through Music

7. The following procedure necessarily applies to Western music. The hope is that once the missionaries becomes aware of the conceptual process in which music is heard in the West, they might be more equipped to discover other conceptual processes. Many musicians are unaware of the way they hear music—the conceptual process resulting from a lifetime of hearing. See chapter 7.

8. I have found it effective in Spanish-speaking areas to illustrate this sensitivity with humorous anecdotes such as the (probably apochryphal) story that in order to wake up Mozart, his wife would play a scale to the seventh note, then stop. He would awaken abruptly, waiting for the eighth, the tonic.

9. These concepts can even be useful in teaching major and minor harmonies if it is remembered that positional degrees may provide color. A change of mode may be viewed as a change of *color*, but *function* within the system relates to relationships within the scale. In the scale of C, the difference in a chord on C Major and C Minor is a difference in *color*, while the difference in a chord on G Major and G Minor is a difference in *function*, for a true dominant to function as dominant in the Germanic tradition of string-of-tension must contain a leading tone! The harmonic minor scale provides *functional* harmonies. The minor subdominant chord is used to darken the mode (a coloring role; it must be remembered that the harmonic form is essentially a product of the Romantic Era). When in history the leading tone came to be used so frequently in minor, the dominant assumed a strong position as tension generator, resolving to tonic. The fact that melodic minor dominated the polyphonic era explains its name.

10. This sequence and procedure, like that of tonal relations, is intended to be suggestive. Effective teaching is a product of creativity.

5

Traditional Methodology in Music Missions

Regarding missionary activity, music itself is not a method. We can no more describe music as a method than we can call the Bible or witnessing a method. Music making, Bible reading, and witnessing are specific activities which, if used in appropriate ways, will hopefully produce certain mission results. This is precisely what the committed missionary wants most—a "handle" which will produce results. A "handle" is simply a specific activity *at hand*, that is, an activity which is feasible in the local environment and within the performance capability of those who will be involved.

Obviously missionaries do read their Bibles and sing their faith, and either activity can be done poorly or effectively. Music methodology, therefore, must concern itself with (1) discovering which particular handles have been used effectively and (2) providing workable procedures for the carrying out of those activities. Applied to music missions, the most useful questions to seek answers for are: "Who should carry out the music work?" "Which musical activities have been most effective?" and "What are useful principles of procedure?"

The weight of Old Testament musical practice was, of course, found in Temple worship where the performers were priests. It may be said that the primary role of the laity in the Old Testament was to stand before the Lord in awe as the leaders invoked and evoked the majesty of God in solemn assembly. Paul was perfectly aware of the massed levitical choirs and orchestras, and while he did not at any

82   Music in Missions: Discipling Through Music

point rule out the role of leadership, he did bring a new and strong emphasis to personal (that is, lay) involvement in musical expression, seen best in the Old Testament and in the Psalms.

We may ask: Why have a music ministry with professional leadership when the first-century church simply sang from the heart whatever happened to be at hand? Indeed, the spiritual Christian might legitimately long for that less complex worship with less sophistication, less admixture of self-exalting egotism, and less mixed motives. Perhaps many sensitive musicians have wondered what worship today might be like if Paul had been allowed personally to supervise the development of church music over two thousand years. We cannot know that, of course, but we can be sure that the practice of worship would be purer. The criteria for composers and performers would place spiritual qualifications above all others, and the spiritual would monitor, prescribe, and regulate the technical qualifications.

But God's hand is freer and grander than the loftiest of missionaries, and today we have more choice than Paul might have given us. We do not have the world of the first century, and we have had no Paul supervising our history. Freedom allows corruption, and although God does not prefer corruption, in His wisdom He does prefer freedom of will, so that our choice of the spiritual will be just that: a choice, valid because it was not coerced.

Because our worship is not pure, if Christ Himself (or Paul) were autocratically to design the worship for a new mission station it is extremely unlikely that He would transport existing models from the West. A new Kikuyu church would probably worship in a form as natural for it as the synagogue model was for the Jerusalem Christians. We can be sure that there would be real excitement over new freedom from sin and from its consequences, over newness in relationship to God, over the thrill of personal holiness, and over the awe and majesty of a fiercely holy, yet warmly loving, Heavenly Father. There would be a high level of spontaneity because of the reality of new life, yet at the same time much of the worship would be ex-

Traditional Methodology in Music Missions 83

pressed in forms that had, for the new Christians, some meaning derived from their lifetime of experiences.

We cannot return to the world of Paul. Good mission methodology seeks not to establish any mode or form but rather to establish a relationship with God through Christ. Worship emerges because people know Christ, not because they know forms or models. Yet the forms or the models are the vehicles with which new converts will worship God, and we must be prepared to utilize those models in the same way Christ would use them as He is calling them into the Kingdom.

Our world is different from the world of Paul, and even the unreached societies lie not far from technology and artificiality, at least geographically. While it is unlikely that the high technology of Western Europe or the United States will penetrate remote tribes in the immediate future, it is also true that computers and automobiles are now found in the most undeveloped of the big cities. Paul's world had fewer resources and less choice regarding models of worship. They did not have pianos or guitars, but they also did not have microphones, building materials such as steel, and videocassettes. Our world is immeasurably more complex; choices are more wide ranging and more difficult. There are questions we cannot now ask and forms we cannot now imitate.

The problem is complicated by the fact that in many missions we inherit traditions gone quite askew. Often a national church will be attempting to worship in forms originally intended to imitate something in the West but practiced by mentalities trained in other modes. The result is often a curious mismatch of Western mode with non-Western practice, producing a form which is unpleasant at best and positively distracting at worst. This is where missionaries can help. The missionary's one great advantage is maturity in the Christian life; most missionaries sincerely want to help national Christians reach the highest level of worship possible to them.

Nita Jones has described Korean Baptist music prior to the recent

84   Music in Missions: Discipling Through Music

innovations and improvements brought by a number of committed
and insightful music missionaries:

> If you had visited a Korean Baptist church prior to 1970, this is what
> you would have observed: Much of the congregational singing was
> off-key. Usually the first stanza would be pretty much on pitch, but
> with each additional stanza, the pitch would climb higher and higher,
> making noticeable discords with the instrument when one was played.
> The tempo of the hymns was slow and draggy - more like a dirge than
> a song of Christian hope. Most of the hymns were Western hymns that
> had been translated (some of them quite poorly) into the Korean
> language. A very small selection of the 586 [hymns] in the Union
> Hymnal, possibly twenty to thirty, was sung over and over again,
> using all the stanzas and many times repeating the same hymn three
> or four times in succession. These hymns were sung with many altera-
> tions in pitch and rhythm. There was usually no one to direct them.
> The pastor standing in the pulpit would "heist" the tune, and the
> congregation would follow him. When accompaniment was present, it
> was on a small pump organ by an accompanist who had little or no
> training. This had the effect of being unaccompanied since the congre-
> gation sang as they pleased, and the accompanist limped along behind!
>
> In the larger churches, there was usually a choir made up of unmar-
> ried young people . . . . Choir development was limited severely by
> untrained directors and accompanists . . .
>
> Directors and accompanists were mostly volunteer. . . . There were
> many students who had studied Beyer methods who could play
> sonatinas, sonatas, preludes, nocturnes, etc., but could not play hymns
> effectively for worship and were very poor sight readers because of
> rote memorization methods they had been subjected to by piano
> teachers. Directors, where they were present, were mostly "time beat-
> ers" with very limited skills in choral conducting.
>
> . . . Percussion was furnished by the pastor who beat rhythmical
> patterns on the pulpit with his hand while singing![1]

Mrs. Jones's description, with minor alterations and additions, is
a valid description of the state of music in the churches of many older
mission fields which have seen little concern for the development of

Traditional Methodology in Music Missions 85

music and understanding of worship. From the musical standpoint alone, the problems she named can be defined: a low level of tonal sensitivity (due to training), uniformity of tempo on all hymns regardless of their character (usually quite slow in most older fields), the use of irrelevant hymns and limited experience in hymns (the same few constantly repeated), frequent lack of accompaniment and where accompaniment is used no relation of the accompaniment to what is sung (lack of sensitivity in the accompaniment, which hinders rather than helps singing), no leadership, and haphazard planning and performance. The sum of it all is that often worship has no direction and meaning, is somewhat unpleasant, and lacks joy in many churches.

A report from Brazil points out other problems missionaries might face regarding physical facilities:

> It is wise to become adaptable to strange situations as quickly as possible. I think in every music clinic which I have conducted or in which I have had a part, from Manaus, 1,000 miles up the Amazon to Belem at its mouth, to Recife, nearest Africa, to Porto Alegre, near Uruguay, in every one, at least one night it has been in the dark, by candlelight .... Most of the people which one teaches in the churches have never had music in their hands, not even a hymnbook with the music. . . . They pitifully can only learn what they can remember and do not grow musically or spiritually because they learn so few new songs.[2]

The peculiarities of dealing with lack of experience, as in the last letter, are pointed up by a letter from Peru: "We have a problem in the new areas as our people wanted to sing the first line of the first stanza, then sing the first line of the second stanza, which was just below it."[3] This lack of experience can extend to create problems in the deepest areas of our Christian lives. A missionary from Japan reported:

> On the mission field, there are limitations all around us: limitations of money and the more serious problem of lack of materials such as

Music in Missions: Discipling Through Music

good, simple anthems in the local language; lack of good religious poetry in Japanese with which to enhance the use of music; lack of technical background among Christian musicians to facilitate the writing of good indigenous hymns; lack of vision on the part of local leaders who cannot know the possibilities of a good music program, and so on and on. Ingenuity is one of the most necessary qualities in a missionary musician, to find a way around these problems. And yet, there is another quality which I would rate even higher—an infinite concern for the understanding of the background and way of thinking of the people among whom one works.

It is true, of course, that people are basically the same everywhere. But because of this we are tempted to assume that patterns of thinking are the same also. This was brought home to me once again recently by a former student, now the pastor of our church, who pointed out that whereas in America young people and adults, as well as children, sing together for fun, there is no such thing as singing for fun in Japan. The school music program teaches children a serious appreciation of good music [but nothing more]. In adulthood, the only group singing is that done at geisha parties where over their *sake* [rice wine] the men sing loudly and clap enthusiastically as the geisha sings and plays the *sami-sen*. Therefore, singing in church, rather than being a spontaneous expression of joy in the Lord, becomes a duty to be performed. This understanding makes some radical differences in one's approach to the development of congregational singing.[4]

So another group of problems can be added to those named above: physical facilities unconducive to musical performance or learning, lack of materials and instruments, lack of experience in handling musical materials (such as the misunderstanding on how to read hymnals with music), lack of vision and appreciation for the role of music, and cultural perspectives which are contrary to a specific Christian orientation (such as the absence of singing together for fun in Japan). Still other problems surface from the experience of many hundreds of missionaries, so numerous, in fact, that it would be impossible to exhaust them with a simple listing of those reported. Some of the more common are: other cultural perspectives which

Traditional Methodology in Music Missions

hinder a specifically Christian orientation (such as the face-saving cultures of the Orient which makes correction in ensembles difficult and, in a different form, makes competition almost impossible in East Africa), a lack of understanding of the nature of congregational participation and unity, differing versions of modesty (such as the fact that in some parts of Africa it is not uncommon to see a mother nursing a baby in the choir), a failure to understand the nature of worship, the problem of working in one area with a number of different languages, and varying terminology and notation (tonic sol-fa in parts of Africa, numeral notation of Western melodies in Chinese-speaking areas, staff notation written backwards in Arabic-speaking areas, the use of fixed-do, and so forth).

This lengthy list of problems does not define the missionary's work in music, however; it only circumscribes it and limits the speed with which true evangelism and worship can develop naturally. The missionary's job is to make disciples, that is, to plant churches and to grow the disciples, that is, to help the churches function in a New Testament way. To those ends one must use music. One's use of music to fulfill those ends is usually called "music promotion"—not the promotion of music but its use in establishing and growing churches. Promotional activities in music missions, therefore, are those activities—training, performance, and assistance in musical participation—which aid and promote national churches in indigenous growth. For convenience, they may be classified as church activities (local and associational), teaching activities, publication, and performance activities.

Church Activities

Missionaries helping churches with their music may work on any number of levels. The largest number includes a vast host of workers who are concentrating on a local church. Some missionaries work with all the churches in an association, that is, they work on an associational level. Others work with an entire state or nation. The latter are roughly equivalent to a state music secretary or a national

88 Music in Missions: Discipling Through Music

music secretary. Principles will remain constant regardless of level although the travel required by these various assignments will vary.

In principle, the actual leadership of a music program should be in the hands of nationals. In practice, many missionaries find themselves forced into positions of leadership either through a vacuum in the personnel available or through personal frustration when leadership does not emerge quickly. Experience teaches that nationals are best in a vast majority of cases: they speak without an accent, their mind-set is compatible with that peculiar expression spiritually and musically appropriate to the culture, and they are not tempted to translate Western concepts or demand Western forms.

But experience has also revealed that occasion arises when a missionary can lead. The leader must be one who can plant indigenous forms. Indigenous expressions will evangelize more successfully, and the results will be more lasting. Obviously a national can always plant indigenous forms more fluently. In very rare cases, missionaries have succeeded in so integrating themselves into the target culture that they lead naturally or almost as naturally as a national.

Two factors are determinant: (1) the greater the psychological distance of a given culture from Western culture, the less likely the missionary will be able to plant indigenous forms. Therefore, in those parts of Africa still dominated by tribal culture, an outsider is extremely unlikely to gain clan acceptance; one's leadership will inevitably implant foreign modes and ideas. In Western Europe, on the other hand, cultures are more in flux. Often, tribal and clan loyalties have disappeared, and an outsider can sometimes become integrated into a group rather quickly. In the Orient, the number of missionaries who adapt to culture easily is likely to be smaller, but some do succeed quickly. (2) The greater the skill of the missionary in language and cultural adaptation, the more likely one is to lead music successfully. Occasionally a missionary will so master the culture and the language, including its idioms, that he or she cannot be easily distinguished from a national.

Traditional Methodology in Music Missions

Congregational Singing

The primary responsibility of any church music leader anywhere is the congregation. A mature congregation will normally have certain characteristics.

1. *Mature Christians understand the nature of worship.* Their expression of it may vary considerably; the fact will not.

2. *In a mature congregation, all or very nearly all will sing regularly.* It is abnormal not to have a song in the heart which seeks outward expression. Their performance will be marked at least by enthusiasm, if not by musical excellence.

3. *Musical performance will be marked by unity.* This does not mean the precision demanded of choral singing, but the spirit of unity finds outward expression in a practiced congruity of performance.

4. *The congregation will understand what it sings, and that understanding will be reflected in its singing.* A thoughtful Christian would not likely sing "Alas, and Did My Savior bleed?" in the same way one would sing "The Church's One Foundation." Fred Allen said that often Zambians do not interpret well because their primary interest is in the musical rather than the verbal.[5]

5. *The congregation will have many hymns in its repertoire.* The pattern is found too often that a few favorites constitute all a congregation knows; see Nita Jone's comments above. This greatly limits their experience of the Christian walk. Some areas (parts of Latin America) sing mainly evangelistic hymns; others (Japan) tend to sing only the majestic hymns (this is recently changing).

6. *The congregation will sing a wide variety of hymns.* They should cover all persons of the Trinity and their work; the complete life and work of Christ are especially important, but the Godhead should be represented fully. A complete hymnody will accomplish all major worship activities: praise, confession, thanksgiving, rejoicing. It will teach major doctrines such as creation, redemption, providence, the church and the kingdom of God, last things. It will praise all the major attributes and works of God: holiness, perfection, purity, power,

majesty, sovereignty, mercy, grace, love, patience, the omniqualities, and so forth. It will contain all the major activities of the Christian life such as fellowship, renewal, ordinances, missions and evangelism, service, social institutions (marriage, family, community, nation), stewardship, prayer.

The absence or weakness of any of these factors may have a number of causes. It may be physical. When Donald Orr began his first term in Colombia, he discovered that there were no hymnals in the pews; at that time, they were family property in that country. However, since each family had only one hymnal, it usually was in the father's hands, and other family members could not sing. Orr made it one of his first projects to attempt to get hymnals into the pews.

It may be due to a lack of training. Many people have never seen a hymnal, and far more have never seen printed music. The layout of the hymn in a musical score may be confusing. Still others are simply oblivious to the defects in poor singing. In Japan, Michael Simoneaux developed, with his pastor's permission, a very effective regular congregational rehearsal. He was able not only to improve their performance but to impart an understanding of the words and their importance.

One of the missionary's main jobs is to train leaders in congregational leadership. This does not mean that missionaries will teach them conducting patterns, although they may do that. It may be the missionary's responsibility to help the nationals discover how they establish downbeats and tempo. Marilyn McMillan, in the Baptist seminary in Tanzania, asked leaders how they established these and helped them define their methods. Rhythmic life is so vital in these areas of East Africa that tempo is established and maintained better by body signals than by hand conducting patterns.

Fred Allen said that one of the more important goals of training is to help the national see the value of a text. In many parts of East Africa, various tribes interchange music so frequently that nationals tend to sing a song in whatever language they learned the song first. Allen attempts to help them see the importance of getting hymns into

Traditional Methodology in Music Missions 91

their own language. He also states that leadership remains in a state of flux with various leaders surfacing at different times of the year, making leadership training quite difficult.[6] Still, its importance is seen in the success of missionaries in many parts of the world.

Church Music Program

The choir can weld a congregation together musically more effectively than any other agency. They also often are the agent that attracts non-Christians to the church. Kent Balyeat reported that he made his choir program a strong point in Argentina because Roman Catholic churches there do not have choir programs, and churchwide choir programs are very attractive to those unfamiliar with their practice.[7]

Rennie Sanderson Ohtani built a model program, a *pilot church*, in Oi Machi Baptist Church in Tokyo which is now directed by a national. A pilot church is a local church in which a fairly complete model of a locally viable music program is developed as an inspiration and a pattern for other churches. Ohtani said that originally her plan was to concentrate on training leaders in Seinan Baptist University, but circumstances changed her direction. Her procedure could well be a classic model for other missionaries to follow who wish to help a church with its music program.

> We realized that until the Japanese saw a live, workable church-music program, they could not [understand its purposes], so when the opportunity came in 1965, I went to Tokyo to the Oi Machi Baptist Church, which is one of ten pilot churches in Japan to develop a pilot music program. During the year, we organized a graded choir program of six choirs—Elementary, Junior High School, Young People-Adult, Women's Chorus, and Men's Chorus. A young man in the church was chosen by the church to work with me in the development of this program. He later became Music Deacon to carry on the program during my absence on furlough.
>
> We chose a representative from each age group to take the responsibility of the choir, and a pianist and helper for each choir. We created

enthusiasm and began teaching the importance of being dependable. Most of the training had to be done on an individual basis. During the first year our music council consisted of a representative from each choir. But finding this an inadequate beginning, the second year we chose a person to be responsible for each of the following areas: congregational singing, choirs, instrumental music (coordinating all accompanists of choirs and congregations), training, publicity and promotion, and secretary. One person who became Music Deacon coordinated and worked with me on the entire program.

The members made their own materials, including flash cards, game song sheets, posters, and so forth. I arranged hymns and did special numbers which were mimeographed. We had piano classes, and classes for song leaders, which later developed into individual training sessions as the pupils advanced. Many were trained individually: song leaders, pianists, organists, choir directors, soloists, officers, and so forth.

Through the leadership of the pastor and a fine Christian lady who directs our kindergarten program, we built our Women's Chorus; it included kindergarten mothers and ladies from the W.M.U. I taught music and English in the kindergarten, and at the end of the year, the children wanted to enter the Children's Choir, so it was necessary to organize an additional choir for them. Each year, because of these additions, the children's choirs have grown. . . .

I gave my leaders individual training. One week I asked the leaders to teach one song to the choir; the second week I added another; the third week I added still another, until soon they were leading all the rehearsals. I sat in the back, taking notes, and at the end of the rehearsal would instruct them. One week I took a trip and left it entirely in their hands. I trained congregational song leaders in the same way—by first letting them lead a song in one of the choirs or one of the Sunday School departments. I let them teach the Hymn-of-the-Month, and activities such as these . . . . I asked them to lead first for an evening service, and then later on Sunday morning.

We trained Junior High School and High School people with talent in the same way—by letting them play and lead one song at choir rehearsal (and similar activities) and then play and lead for a retreat,

Traditional Methodology in Music Missions 93

the High School Revival, or something of like nature. From this came some leaders for our children's choirs as well as one dedication for full-time Christian service.

In October of 1965 we had a music school for our church, but because of requests from other churches, we invited any who wished to come. . . . Many came from Tokyo and Yokohama, and even one from out of the area. We described our program to them. I let the leaders of the choirs themselves tell how we had developed the program. The school provided classes and training for all these areas. Out of these came enthusiasm and requests for help in other churches.[8]

Not all situations will have the ideal cooperation of the pastor and laypersons of the church as Ohtani had. Physical circumstances will vary greatly, and the local cultural model may require radically different modes and forms. In Africa, the choir may be a circle. The leader in many parts of Africa is not always the one standing in front of the congregation; a woman in the audience may assume the role. They often have twice as many persons on a row, and so they sing better because they touch each other. Rhythm, so vital in Africa, is communicated by touch.

In underdeveloped countries, churches may have no lights, so meetings are best scheduled during daylight hours. Circumstances and cultural modes vary so greatly that it is virtually impossible to program a specific kind of development, but some kind of program (such as ensembles instead of choirs) is likely to be feasible in most situations.

Worldwide, churches suffer from lack of accompanists. Their recruitment and training should be a major goal of missionaries hoping to help with music. David Brazzeal has been a home music missionary, working with the Puget Sound Baptist Association headquartered in Seattle. He reported:

A project that has been the long-time dream of several small churches and missions in our area will be coming to fruition this month. A number (probably ten percent) of our churches have no accompanists for their worship services. They have been requesting cassette tape accompaniments to hymns so that their congregations may praise the Lord together in song. We have been reluctant to produce such an "electronic hymnal," imagining the worst as someone fumbled to locate specific hymns on the tape while the congregation waited in awkward silence—not a very worshipful scene.

One solution that we hope will prove workable and worshipful is to record hymns not in numerical order but by subject matter (grace, second coming, Easter, and so forth). Three hymns for a service plus an offertory and invitation will be on one tape. The tape player will only have to be turned on and off at the appropriate times. Since the hymns will be related and corresponding Scriptures will be suggested, the tapes will also be an indirect way of promoting more effective and thoughtful worship planning.[9]

This ingenious solution might be helpful to other missionaries working in those many areas where accompanists are not to be found. However, a tape cannot be sensitive to the personality of a local congregation (although most accompanists in training are far from being able to adjust to a particular body of people; they are happy if they get the notes). In the long run, training accompanists must be the more important goal.

Missionaries working over wider geographical areas will need to schedule trips to the various churches. Specific work in a given church must always come by invitation. Missionaries should acquaint the churches of their area with their willingness to help and the possibilities inherent in a music program.

Teaching Activities

The training of laypersons in clinics, workshops, institutes, and church programming is the most frequently reported teaching activity in churches; music workshops, under whatever name, are universally reported. This is quite natural in view of the strong New Testament emphasis on personal expression in music. Enthusiastic reception is reported in both urban and rural settings, in highly literate and in underdeveloped cultures, in young churches and in

Traditional Methodology in Music Missions 95

long-established ones. Whatever sharpening of musical skill is offered is almost always seized with alacrity.

The most frequently included subject is music reading under a large variety of names: music theory, sightsinging, music fundamentals, solfege, and so forth. There seems to be an instinctive demand for a tool in hand to aid in the preservation of learned materials, as well as for learning new music. The success of this subject in clinics is unquestionable and should always be a prime vehicle for developing church music programs.

Techniques of teaching reading or fundamentals is generally accomplished by lecture, demonstration, and exercises, with several missionaries having developed their own very effective materials (Jim Castlen, Philippines; Debbie Weber, Taiwan; Barbara Deal, Colombia; Fred Allen, Zambia, to name a few.). One effective method of teaching tonal relations is found in James C. McKinney's *The Beginning Music Reader*, available in several other languages. This method associates musical interval with numerical "space" and deserves increasing use. It can also be related to musical experience; in McKinney's book, known hymns serve as a point of departure for the interval training. Once McKinney's method is understood, missionaries could select hymns well known in their own countries. No one system of teaching rhythm predominates, and generally the point of departure in rhythmic reading seems to be notation itself.

Training in tonal reading and tonal sensitivity usually precedes rhythmic reading. The level of instruction should be on the level of the local experience. Many clinics have included much singing of choruses and easy music; as many musical experiences as possible should be provided a given constituency, providing a store of musical awareness on which to base training in reading when the teaching of reading becomes feasible.

Another area nearly always included in music workshops is a choir session. This is of unquestionable importance and value because the multiplication of experience develops much needed sensitivity and musical consciousness. It provides an opportunity to introduce reper-

96   Music in Missions: Discipling Through Music

toire (or to such as is available). In some places, this class hour is given to training in congregational singing, again, the most basic musical responsibility of the missionary. The choir session is a good setting for teaching choral technique, and in fact, it is sometimes labeled "choral techniques." In stations where some church members may have musical appetites and abilities above the average, this training offers the advantage of learning how to sharpen performance.

Hymnology is included less often; it will usually interest those who already have some background in music fundamentals. Many local courses in hymnology are concerned with hymn stories. Ideally, they would also concern themselves with content (theology, the scope of a given text, and so forth) and language (meter, imagery, and so forth). However, the stories are valuable in capturing interest, and at times they may serve evangelistic purposes.

> At a recent music workshop in Achupallas, Chile, there were two decisions to accept Christ as Savior. Lee Walker, music missionary, shares that in the teaching of two hymns he included something of the salvation experience of the hymnwriter and as a result, two people decided to accept Christ.[10]

Many missionaries report classes on music in worship and on the biblical bases for music. These are valuable where congregational participation in public worship is minimal, or where the role of music is not understood. It has the additional advantage of demonstrating another area of reliance on biblical models. Other areas included in lay music clinics are voice, accompaniment, and conducting, but these properly belong under leadership training.

The most critical problems (outside of teaching method itself) in music clinics are (1) materials and (2) equipment. While these problems are not as severe as they were a decade ago, they are still persistent in many parts of the world. The usual solution is for the missionary or talented nationals to improvise both, that is, to develop and duplicate their own teaching materials or their own anthems

Traditional Methodology in Music Missions

(usually hymn arrangements). Prior training in composition and arranging would be helpful. Here again, practical experience, along with a determined rugged self-criticism, may be the best teacher. Missionaries should learn to use portable instruments: guitars, accordions, autoharps, melodicas, and the like. Locally made instruments are more likely to come from woods and materials that will withstand local climates; they are inexpensive enough that when they are broken or meet an untoward fate, their replacement is not a major budget item. Teaching aids such as dummy keyboards, where appropriate, may be improvised.

Second in importance to the training of laypersons is the training of lay leaders; the training of leadership inevitably becomes a major responsibility as churches grow and musical practice develops. Many music clinics for the lay constituency of the church include classes which technically are for leaders—accompanying, conducting, and the like. Where classes in these areas are not yet feasible, it is the music leader's job to stimulate development and provide musical experiences which will finally make even leadership classes useful.

Many church bodies now have national music organizations associated with them (Japan, Brazil, Korea, Argentina, and so forth). At the time of its organization, the National Baptist Music Congress of Argentina had a twelve-member executive committee with three active subcommittees: a bulletin committee, a concert committee, and a music institute committee. The latter was under the aegis of the National Baptist Music Commission and has conducted a number of ambitious institutes that included choir directing, children's choir leadership, guitar, voice, and organ. The institute lasts three months and covers a metropolitan or associational area.

Gary McCoy of Korea wrote:

> The major emphasis of each [music] missionary's work is on training national music leaders for ministry in the local church. Since 1970 the number of churches in Korea has more than doubled, to about 800. As a result of this growth there are acute shortages of choir directors and

98   Music in Missions: Discipling Through Music

accompanists. In the four cities where there are music missionaries, the general approach is to offer a ten-week study course for the lay music directors once a year in the fall and then in the spring a similar course for accompanists.

These study courses meet once a week for a two- to three-hour period. The study content includes music theory, sightsinging, conducting technique, and other necessary subject matter as needs are recognized. The accompanists spend much time on applied service playing and piano technique in addition to theory studies. The missionary is the main teacher assisted by the national employee, as well as recognized guest musicians. If the lay musician has attended all the sessions, he will receive from 25 to 35 hours of basic music training. The last session usually includes a fellowship time and certificates are awarded. Since the first course of this nature in 1976, several hundred have enrolled in these courses and the level and depth of study have steadily increased.[11]

Another kind of teaching activity has recently become prominent: music camps. Like lay leadership institutes, music camps are feasible only where the church has a secure foothold: it is older, enjoys a fairly secure place in society, and is financially independent from a foreign board; camps require an attendance large enough to justify the effort and the expense. The camps are fairly recent appearance on the mission scene; their utility has caused rapid expansion of their use, and their use is now reported in many countries on all continents.

They have the advantage of providing a retreat setting. A people drawn apart can more readily concentrate on the Lord, will more positively relate music to service, will be less easily distracted from the immediate learning task, and will enjoy a degree of camaraderie not usually found in the weekly choir practice. In some cases (for example, Argentina), a music camp has been combined with a conference on some other area such as religious education. Milton Lites, in Taiwan, placed the emphasis on youth. The annual music camp in Denia, Spain, has drawn a number of the more recognized musicians

Traditional Methodology in Music Missions   99

of some areas of Spain. The camp choir gave concerts in nearby cities and towns with auspicious publicity breakthroughs.

One problem of camps is finding a suitable location. Some countries (Kenya and Spain) have church campgrounds. Larry Rice (Venezuela) solved the problem by having a camp on the seminary campus. Attendance at the latter was promoted by well-planned brochures distributed through the churches.

One last kind of teaching activity which is quite productive is that which is accomplished through festivals. "Festival" is a generic term for any large gathering of believers in which Christian song becomes a major activity. Often they are choir festivals (Barbara Deal, Colombia; Milton Lites, Taiwan), sometimes with prepared choir numbers submitted for adjudication. This has been practiced for many years in Nigeria where no music missionary specialist has yet (1985) been appointed.

Mission situations frequently dictate that area-wide festivals be just that: a festive gathering of praise song. In Spain, area music festivals are basically an occasion for fellowship, with ensembles and soloists from the churches presenting music for listening rather than adjudication; congregational song is an important part of these meetings. In addition to his biannual choir festivals, Fred Allen led the Zambian National *Evangelistic* Conference to include a songfest in which nineteen choirs participated; the songfest was scheduled for 10:30 on Saturday night, and, although it ended "officially" at 12:15 AM, the actual singing continued until daybreak. Carolyn Houts called the festivals in Ghana a "Choir Day":

> We had a good Kumasi Choir day in June [1984]. Three hundred people were involved as choirs from nine churches sang songs they had practiced. We sang hymns and also learned a new hymn that morning to sing together as a massed choir . . . . The musicians were thrilled with the experience and began asking, "When will the next Choir Day be held?"[14]

It is evident that the festal nature of such occasions provides an

100 Music in Missions: Discipling Through Music

opportune occasion for musical expression and thus for musical growth.

Publication

Ultimately any national Christian group must develop an adequate program of music publication if national development proceeds so rapidly that printed materials are a live option for the Christian constituency of a nation. By 1985, a significant proportion of the countries of the world had some kind of publishing facilities. Some of these are well established and may be considered models of what should ideally appear as musical practice develops in the churches: Baptist Press, Hong Kong; Jordan Press, Tokyo; the Casa de Publicaciones, El Paso; the Junta Bautista de Publicaciones, Buenos Aires; and the Junta de Educacao Relgiosa e Publicacoes, Rio de Janeiro, to name a few.

The hymnal is the primary musical tool of any missionary. Normally, a word hymnal, with stanzas printed as poetic strophes, is preferable. It has advantages which should not be overlooked, even in well-developed areas: it reveals content and poetry more readily; it is cheaper; it does not require specialized processes of preparation of copy and reproduction.

Nevertheless, a hymnal with music is indispensable for music training and ultimately for the more efficient learning of new tunes. If one is not available, music clinics and lay training are seriously hampered. A word hymnal is first priority for the planting of churches and discipleship; a music hymnal is necessary for later continued development.

The most difficult problem in publishing hymnals is finding satisfactory indigenous hymns. Sometimes nationals and missionaries overlook some of the native forms available. (This will be discussed more fully in chapter 7). Darrell Mock has pointed out the suitability of *tanka* poetic verse in Japanese:

> The *tanka* is a poetic verse of 5-7-5-7-7 (thirty-one syllables) which

Traditional Methodology in Music Missions   101

is from the ancient past of Japan. Pastor Ushimaru . . . feels that the
use of this form, which is familiar to the Japanese and is wedded to
their language, could give rise to hymns which are poetically beautiful,
biblically sound, and verbally understood . . .

People are being encouraged today to write the thirty-one syllable
tanka hymn verses and sing them. It gives an opportunity to witness
their faith when their own hymns are sung by the group during a
worship service. Seiki Tasaka, Professor of Japanese Classical literature
at Aoyama Gakuin Methodist University, draws a parallel with the
indigenization of Buddhism in Japan. It was not until Buddhist chants,
originally "kansan," developed into "wansan" and "imayo" about the
tenth century that Buddhism really took root in Japan. "Kansan" were
imported chants or hymns of praise, based on Chinese characters,
listened to [rather than sung] by the people. "Wansan" were the Japanese translations which could be sung by the people. "Imayo" was an
ancient verse form of four lines (7-5-7-5- syllables). The Christian
church would do well to make use of an indigenous form of poetry
which has shown such enduring qualities.[12]

Not all indigenous forms will derive from ancient classical models.
The *coritos* of Latin America and Spain and the *choeurs* of West Africa
and France are closely wedded to similar secular folk songs. Jerry
Robertson described the form as practiced in Ivory Coast:

But when African Christians sing most meaningfully, they sing
choeurs, or songs of the heart, that are not in any book. In this sort of
music Robertson found a rich tradition of Christian hymns that had
developed from the wellspring of their own experience.

He collected 90 such songs on tape in a three-month period and
decided there so many he couldn't get them all. "When I ask people
where a song comes from, some say, 'Nobody wrote it,' or 'I heard it
from a friend who heard it somewhere else.' And so it has just kind
of developed," points out Robertson. "There is a hymnody here in
Ivory Coast; it's just not written down. It is a treasury of songs that
everybody knows, and they teach them to one another."[13]

Another source of indigenous hymns may be stimulated by re-

102   Music in Missions: Discipling Through Music

ward; some missionaries have been able to encourage national church bodies to sponsor hymn-writing contests. These may be local (Rennie Ohtani in the Tokyo area) or national. William McElrath led the *Suara Baptis,* a bimonthly Baptist magazine in Indonesia, to sponsor a contest which resulted in the publication of a pocket-size hymnal which was probably the largest collection every published of hymns written entirely by Indonesian Christians. Twenty of the twenty-five hymns in the hymnal were new at the time; they were written by editors, a postal employee, a volunteer choir leader, four Baptist pastors, a bookkeeper, a secretary, a pastor's wife, and a missionary.[15]

Hymnals need not wait to be published in final form if there exists such a need for new hymns that it is more helpful to publish sections periodically in partial form, or even simply to publish small books. The Indonesian hymnal of 1980 was preceded by such "installments." Glenn Boyd influenced the national church body in Tanzania to publish a booklet, *Tufurahi na Kuimba* ["Rejoice and Sing"] with matching cassette so that nationals could learn the tunes.[16]

The pattern in the past has been that hymnals published outside Europe and North America have tended to be careless about (or to ignore) credits and titles. In recent years this tendency has been changed, largely through the influence of music missionaries. Such a large number of hymnals have appeared or are now in progress that it would be impossible to name them all. Carolyn Houts published an excellent hymnal in the Twi language in Ghana in 1980; Gerald Workman is currently (1985) supervising an ambitious revision of the Chichewa hymnal in Malawi.

The most recent edition of the *Cantor Cristao,* edited by William Ichter in Brazil, contains all indices and some new tunes and hymn settings. Edward Nelson edited a very ambitious *Himnario Bautista* at the Spanish Baptist Publishing House in El Paso, published in 1978, that included all credits, all indices, more than one-hundred indigenous songs procured from all parts of the Spanish-speaking world, and an extensive section of worship helps. The hymnal committees were broadly based, coming from all parts of the Spanish-speaking

Traditional Methodology in Music Missions 103

world. Another monumental effort in recent mission history is the *New Songs of Praise* in Chinese, published in Hong Kong in 1974 with L. G. McKinney as its editor. Like the *Himnario Bautista*, this was an entirely new hymnal, with a large number of indigenous hymns as well as hymn tunes, and was a result of the cooperation of a committee drawn from the entire Chinese-speaking world, including Mandarin and Cantonese. The committee was extraordinarily scrupulous in comparing and selecting translations, as well as in its standards for indigenous poetry and music.[17]

Decisions on what to include should be based on relevance and need rather than whim. A thick book costs more. Ideally, the hymnal will be within the price range of nationals; even in countries where the churches, rather than individuals, buy the hymnals, indigenization is hampered by expensive hymnals. In some areas, early hymnals may well be paperback; they are expendable anyway. Paperback word hymnals are especially common in Africa; as literacy and national development proceed, hardback hymnals with music begin to make their appearance. One hymnal is often used by several different denominations and church groups.

Readable preparation of copy, as distinct from reproduction, has improved rapidly in recent years, especially in those countries which have a late-model music typewriter. Preparation of copy may be by manuscript although this tends to be uneven in its quality and penmanship. Recently several software companies have produced programs for music notation, but many of these are not compatible with some of the more common printers, and the quality is that of dot-matrix printing. This problem will probably be overcome very soon, and computer preparation will no doubt be much faster than the use of a music typewriter. Still another procedure that has been used in music mission printing is the pasting together of photographs of hymns from various sources. The result is a motley quality that discourages reading; uniformity of print and appearance encourage reading.

Some countries use a dual notation in their hymnals, especially

Chinese-speaking areas and Indonesia which use both staff and numeral notation and, in some cases, African countries which use staff and tonic sol-fa notation. Both numeral and tonic sol-fa notation are essentially a vocal notation, and nationals read these with facility. However, both are awkward for rhythmic reading, and staff notation is better suited for instrumental reading.

The missionary will also need some printed anthems and arrangements. This lacuna was quite serious only a short time ago, but materials have become available in major languages such as Japanese, Spanish, Portuguese, and Indonesian. In other areas, the field of printed Christian music is a virtual desert. Even in several of the major language areas, those workers responsible for what has already been printed report that they are unable to meet the rapidly expanding needs of their churches. Some missionaries have solved this problem by translating American anthems, stripping in the words, and reproducing them. The 1973 Conference on Church Music for Asia in Manila, Philippines voted to make a strong statement on violation of copyright, and especially since that time missionaries have been more scrupulous to obtain permission from American publishers.

A better solution is for the missionary to secure the offices of someone capable of producing arrangements congenial to the mindset of the area and to reproduce them. A few missionaries are sufficiently bi-musical to compose idiomatically in the national idiom. The best solution of all, of course, is to encourage nationals to produce their own music. This is one of the most serious challenges facing missionaries who work with music. John McGuckin in Argentina asked for cassette recordings of songs by talented nationals; the more promising of these were transcribed, edited, and published in the series *Corazón y Voz* ("Heart and Voice"). Edward Nelson gathers Latin American songs through extensive travel in Spanish-speaking areas and publishes these in the series *Cante al Señor*.

Prose materials are greatly needed; at present they exist only in the major languages named above. Japan has an excellent series of handbooks on church music; Brazil has good hymnology studies; the

Traditional Methodology in Music Missions 105

Spanish Baptist Publishing House is the oldest of the mission publishing houses to produce handbooks and it has the largest collection available, including books on music ministry and hymnody. Brazil enjoys the presence of more Baptist music missionaries than any other country; the music development there is now far enough along to warrant rather advanced writing and mature contributions. Boyd Sutton has been the chairman of a committee of the Organization of Brazilian Baptist Musicians which presented to the national body in January of 1985 a "Philosophy of Brazilian Baptist Church Music."[18] Sandy Simmons, teaching at the Girls' Training School and the Baptist seminiary in Rio de Janeiro, is writing a textbook on the history of church music.[19]

Denominational organs and church papers provide convenient outlets for informing the constituency of developments and of the availability of materials and personnel. For several years, William Ichter published a regular column, "Canto musical," in *O Jornal Batista,* national newspaper of Brazilian Baptists. A similar column, *Cofre Armónico,* appears in *El Promotor* from the Spanish Baptist Publishing House. Phil Anderson has at times placed inserts in Sunday School materials in the Philippines to inform churches of musical possibilities and developments.

Secular publications can also serve the missionary's purposes. Musical events offer more potential than any other activity for gaining the ear of the press. The well-known breakthrough accomplished by Donald Orr's first production of *Messiah* in Colombia in 1964 (see chapter 1) is a landmark in music-mission history. Community service projects often bring Christian work to the attention of the news media; Orr's production was by a community chorus, and proceeds from the performance were given to the local symphony fund. The success of the performance gained considerable local approval and notoriety; after such breakthroughs, other projects are more palatable to the press.

The order of importance for capturing attention in secular publications is normally: a picture, the headline, the article. The missionary cannot choose the headline; he or she can make the picture. After the 1964 *Messiah* in Cali, a picture appeared in the leading local newspaper of Orr presenting a check to the director of the symphony of the proceeds from the concert.

Performance Activities

The most successful of the performance activities continues to be united choirs. James Castlen has a "Baguio Baptist Chorale," made up of singers from the Philippine Baptist Theological Seminary and from the Baguio City Baptist Churches. Donald Snell directs a group assembled from the three Baptist churches of Bermuda which presented a cantata at Easter in 1984 and netted ten decisions for Christ. Betty Dixon works with a National Youth Choir in Angola; she wrote:

> After only three good practices, they presented—in four parts— "Glorious Is Thy Name" and "My God and I" to the whole [National Youth] Congress. Their faces radiated the joy in their hearts. Presently, everything is by rote except for a very few who can play a small electric or pump organ. As they eventually learn to read music, we hope they will be motivated to put their own compositions down on paper.[20]

L. G. McKinney has directed the Hong Kong Choral Society in several major works: *Elijah, St. Paul,* the Brahms *Requiem,* and Haydn's *Seasons* and *Creation.* An imaginative use of large choirs was Fred Spann's 110-voice choir organized in Recife, Brazil, to celebrate the three hundred and fifty-first anniversary of the Protestant Reformation; the local symphony accompanied.

Smaller ensembles are useful for tours and, in some cases, have served evangelistic purposes with encouraging results. Edward Steele led six groups of seventy-three singers and instrumentalists to tour three interior cities of Panama. He stated, "Each group sang, played, and shared testimonies, in addition to a leader from the youth organization preaching a short message, leading many to hear the gospel for the first time."[21] Jerry Robertson is part of a six-member music evan-

Traditional Methodology in Music Missions 107

gelism group in Abidjan, Ivory Coast, called "Union." Seminary teacher Jorge Sedaca, an Argentine, organized a youth chorus in Buenos Aires which has had outstanding results: in nine concerts, the group saw around 175 decisions for Christ.[22] Smaller ensembles have the advantages of requiring smaller budgets and producing musical results more quickly.

Solo recitals present certain practical advantages: missionaries control all rehearsal time; they control the content of oral testimony; they can utilize the opportunity to inform and interest church leaders in the ministry of music. A strong caution is necessary: Western church music threatens the growth of indigenous expression in many parts of the world. Success or failure depends on the peculiar situation of the local culture. In nations such as Spain concerts have proved to be useful. The crucial factor does not seem to be charisma alone but a sense of timing and of appropriateness in the local setting.

A growing number of handbell choirs are reported on all continents, and in every case missionaries report a delighted reaction. This is astonishing in view of the fact that handbell choirs are so thoroughly English in origin. Oriental orchestras often have bell-like instruments including gongs and various percussion instruments, and success might be predictable, say, in Malaysia or Indonesia. The expense is usually an insurmountable obstacle; a number of the sets now in use were given by churches or state conventions in the United States.

A few missionaries have been successful in composing and arranging. The most prolific writer until now has been Joan Sutton, who grew up in Brazil and whose grasp of the language and mind-set is thoroughly natural. She has created for herself and her mission a notable reputation with her works. They include many arrangements, songs, translations, art music, and a cantata, *E Habitou Entre Nós*; many of them are published. Such activity provides much-needed materials as well as a specific example of the kinds of possibilities available to native composers. It is probably no accident that Brazil is now producing some excellent composers of church music.

108   Music in Missions: Discipling Through Music

Many missionary musicians have occasion to participate in radio and television work from time to time, although only a small number work on a continuing basis in media. Those who have to prepare music for regular weekly programs usually establish a regular recording choir or ensemble. Ideally these should consist of committed Christian musicians who live within traveling distance of the recording studio since frequent rehearsal is mandatory. One of the earliest problems a musician working in media must face is the recruitment of available talent who will work faithfully in rehearsals. Larry Rice in Venezuela has had outstanding success with a group whose records are popular in the Spanish-speaking world.

Special occasions frequently provide opportunity to secure air time. Fred Spann stated:

> Now when the seminary [in Recife] has a good program, cantata, etc., to present, we call up channel two and they give us prime time . . . . for up to an hour's program. They have even hired their videotape crew to record these programs when it was not convenient for the choir to come at the best playing time . . . these programs are given to us. They would cost commercially around Cr$1,500,000.[23]

Recordings of discs, cassettes, and tapes have also proved a valuable ministry. Cassettes have been used as learning aids with new songbooks. It was reported that ten thousand requests for cassette copies of music and sermon programs came during 1983 as a result of weekly radio programs in Venezuela.[24] Recordings are expensive and require exhaustive rehearsal plus long difficult hours of recording, but the product is permanent and can be repeated by the national (or by a missionary) at will.

Creative Methodology

There remains an enormous amount of music missionary activity which defies classification, yet which is imaginative and effective. June Cooper led the Japan Baptist Convention to have a "Church Music Year" in 1973. Planning started in 1969 with the first meeting

Traditional Methodology in Music Missions

of the national Church Music Committee. The Japan Baptist Convention is divided into thirteen area associations. Music promotors were chosen for these associations, made up of ten musical laypersons and three professional (non-church) musicians. The promotors selected the theme for the Church Music Year—in rough translation: "Let's all sing the songs of our heart, songs of faith!" Nineteen-seventy-one and 1972 were years of preparation. A hymn-writing contest was set for October, 1972, and a handbook was prepared to be released during 1973. A logo was chosen, and rubber stamps of it were distributed to the area promotors to use on correspondence and publicity materials:

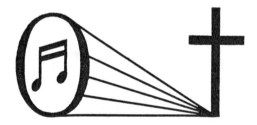

Figure 1. Japan Church Music Year Symbol

Teams were assigned to travel and teach at various meetings during the year; to conserve travel funds, one team covered two areas. Some of the areas had one-day meetings, and others had two- or three-day meetings. The Fukuoka meeting in south Japan was held in two sections: an evangelistic music festival on Saturday before the meeting on Sunday. At this evangelistic festival, two made decisions for baptism, twenty-two to become seekers, and five to become choir members.[25]

Additional projects can be named from all over the mission world. In 1980 Larry Rice in Venezuela formed a National Baptist Orchestra

110　　　　　　　　Music in Missions: Discipling Through Music

with fourteen members. In the Bahamas Mike and Gloria Hudson do puppet shows with music. Taipei has a Church Music Center. The list could not be exhaustive, but the creativity should be suggestive, and indicates the kind of work into which God's Holy Spirit leads His children. The creative power of music continues to stimulate His children to become more like their own creative God.

Notes

1. Nita Jones, "Korean Baptist Music Before 1970," *Missionary Notes*, July 1977, p. 1.

2. Unsigned questionnaire, Jan.-Mar. 1967.

3. Unsigned questionnaire, Jan.-Mar., 1967.

4. Jean P. Shepard, letter to the author, 9 Feb. 1967.

5. Fred Allen, guest class lecture, Music in Missions class, Southwestern Baptist Theological Seminary, 23 Jan. 1975.

6. *Ibid.*

7. Kent Balyeat, guest class lecture, Music in Missions class, Southwestern Baptist Theological Seminary, 30 Jan. 1975. Balyeat is now deceased.

8. Rennie Sanderson Ohtani, "The Church Music Program at Oi Machi," monograph written for the Music in Missions class at Southwestern Baptist Theological Seminary, 1967, pp. 3-5. Regarding her role of leadership, a number of Japanese nationals have stated that Ohtani speaks unusually fluent and idiomatic Japanese and understands Japanese customs thoroughly.

9. David Brazzeal, Missionary Newsletter, Sept.-Oct. 1984, p. 2.

10. Catherine Walker, "Called to Pray," prayer bulletin of the Foreign Mission Board, Southern Baptist Convention, 5 Oct. 1984, p. 3.

11. Gary W. McCoy, "Music Mission Trends Among Korean Baptists," *Southern Baptist Church Music Journal*, Jan. 1984, p. 28.

12. Darrell Mock, "Hymnology in Japan and Its Problems," unpublished monograph, Oct. 1984. Mock was a music missionary to Japan.

13. Jim Newton and Mike Creswell, "Ivory Coast: Where the Music's Fresh," *The Commission*, Nov. 1980, pp. 27-28.

14. Carolyn Houts, Missionary Newsletter, Dec. 1984.

15. "Indonesian Christians Write Hymns for Pocket Hymnal," News Release, Foreign Mission Board, Southern Baptist Convention, 23 Feb. 1978.

16. "Music Missionary News," *Missionary Notes*, Sept. 1975, p. 3.

17. See Britt E. Towery, Jr., "New Songs of Praise," *The Commission*, Apr. 1971, pp. 10-11, for a more complete description of this hymnal.

18. Boyd Sutton, Missionary Newsletter, 22 Nov. 1984.

Traditional Methodology in Music Missions

19. Sandy Simmons, Missionary Newsletter, 12 Apr. 1984. In mission areas, most church-music books have been translations. New works with an emphasis on local and national history is a great need.

20. Curtis and Betty Dixon, Missionary Newsletter, Dec. 1984.

21. Edward Steele, Missionary Newsletter, 18 Sept. 1984.

22. Jorge Sedaca, Circular newsletter, Apr. 1984.

23. Letter from Fred Spann to the author, 6 Oct. 1966. No attempt has been made to revise the currency conversion from the 1966 value.

24. "Ministering through the Media," *The Commission*, May 1984, 37.

25. June Cooper, "The Japan Music Year" report presented to the Conference on Church Music for Asia, Nov. 1973, pp. 1-17.

6

Indigenous Music

One of the most anfractuous problems missionaries face is the problem of indigenous music. Most missionaries have a vague conviction that they ought to use indigenous music, but they feel considerable discomfort about the methodology, uncertainty about the extent of pressure they ought to bring, and find it a bit uncongenial in their own experience anyway.

Still, missionaries are usually the ones who choose what kind of music will be sung in developing areas. William Supplee has pointed out that missionaries are taking eight basic paths in their approach to music in mission areas: (1) European music is the only good church music. (2) Missionaries should use contemporary gospel songs. (3) Missionaries avoid native expressions in favor of the songs of Sankey. (4) Adapt European songs and melodies to the pentatonic scale. (5) Accept the fact that some people "just cannot sing." (6) Assume that the local music is sinful. (7) Use existing tunes in the language of the people. (8) Allow the nationals to compose music for the church in their own idioms.[1]

Supplee has advocated the latter two for a number of years. With new strategies available as a result of education in anthropology and ethnic studies, missionaries have more leeway today to encourage the use of indigenous music than at any time in the history of Christianity. The choice is a real one.

In general terms, with reference to indigenous music there are three situations most missionaries might face. The first of these is that

Indigenous Music 113

remote area or tribe where the people have had little contact with the outside world; the musical experience of the target group will be simply their own heritage. They will know little or nothing about the music of other cultures. The second situation will involve a people in contact with national, as well as local, trends, a people who will have some experience on radio and cassette of other musics, and who have a certain though limited choice in the kind of music they want to sing, their own or "foreign." The third situation touches people with a very wide variety of experience in musical culture: experience of their own music, the songs of other tribes or communities, and likely even Western music. The latter are likely to be urban or have considerable contact with urban areas. These categories are arbitrary, of course, and are intended only to provide a general basis for discussion.

Practically, however, most mission situations will approximate one of these. For convenience, let us call these *pioneer*,[2] *syncretistic*, and *urban*. The first and third represent work in extreme conditions—work with people who have never heard any music but their own, who are virtually isolated as opposed to work with people whose experience is quite universal. The middle group represents mild syncretism—people to whom one musical style is more congenial but who also are influenced by contact with outsiders. Foreign missions will involve all three of these situations. Home missions (contained within a Western cultural environment) will deal mainly with the second and third; pockets of indigeneity (for example, Black music or Indian music in the United States) will fall somewhere in the framework of categories two and three.

Pioneer Areas

Surely there can be no question that the only viable music for unreached peoples is their own. The missionary's first efforts in music should involve the same respect for their musical system and its position and function in culture as for their language. Missionaries cannot communicate at all unless they know their vocabulary, grammar, and pronunciation. But they learn quickly that language is far more than words, rules, and mouth shapes. Language reflects every aspect and part of culture. Missionaries want to see how language functions, how its idioms reflect local life-style and peculiarities of thinking, how elastic and how specific is the vocabulary in its various combinations, contexts, and situations. They will become sensitive to new kinds of humor, word plays, relationships, expressions of status or contempt, courtesies, and formalities. The desire to use the local language in all its idiosyncrasies is, I assume, the normal and natural desire of any serious missionary.

The factors dealing with language are also true in the music of the people the missionary is working with. Just as their own jokes are funny, it is their own music that "really" marries them, speeds up the canoeing, or expresses their fears, joys, and worship. *Missionaries in this situation will find their primary responsibility to be encouraging local musicians, singers, performers, and, if possible, composers to produce and perform appropriate music in a style natural to the people.* The problem of appropriateness will require a great deal of sensitivity as well as trust in the Holy Spirit and the instincts of new Christians. The missionary will, of course, associate music with the ramifications of their new life in Christ, the meaning of spiritual worship, the new character they have in Christ, and His demands for holiness in living. Their spiritual instincts need to be brought under the discipline of the Holy Spirit and the limits imposed by the Bible within the context of its application to culture.

Culture

Here we stumble into the knottiest and most resistant problem we have. Is culture a good to be preserved, an evil to be transformed, or yet a third thing not utterly black or white? There has never been a truly Christian culture. By definition, culture is an expression of all that is human. If we are serious at all about our Christianity, sooner or later we have to face the fact that since culture is a human expression, it will contain, indeed probably will be dominated by, what the Bible calls "the flesh." The sincerely seeking Christian will probably

Indigenous Music
115

have to admit that the tendency of most Western cultures—from the standpoint of the Bible—is downward.

Historically, in periods of renewal, Christianity has had beneficial effects on many cultures. At times it has had a purifying effect and has stimulated new works and new expressions of culture, for example the German chorale at the time of the Reformation and the chorale arrangements of Bach after Pietism had gained so much ground. The power of renewal in these periods was often countered in subsequent generations by the stultifying effect of an institutionalizing of the cultural product. What was in one generation a statement so fresh that it had an improvisatory flavor became in the next generation a classic with rigid rules of performance. The cultural product was itself substituted for the freshness of spirit that originally produced it.

But these brief periods of refreshment cannot brake the huge lumbering wave of the totality of culture. The total culture (for example, in the West) compasses a literature which delights in picturing the ribald privacy of society's seamier members, paintings which denigrate by revealing what should be glorified by hinting, music which laughs at the holy and sanctifies the ridiculous, not to mention the folk arts of bawdy humor, character assassination, rumor mongering, and fence poetry. If Western culture is typical of the tendency of culture in general, then as society advances, it becomes increasingly fashionable to deify the mundane while stripping the rights of privacy from graciousness, majesty, and holiness.

This is not intended to be a critic's diatribe against the tendencies of Western civilization. I am not a critic and have nothing to offer those minds far greater than mine which evaluate the intricacies of communication and which preserve for history a picture of what our world is like and is becoming. I speak only to the church, and even there not as a trained theologian but as an observer, a learner, and a follower of One who was utterly separated from the entrenched powers dominating His own culture.

Yet I am hoping to speak to a very important arm of the church,

116   Music in Missions: Discipling Through Music

to those men and women carrying His message to the unreached. We who encounter people in cultures radically unlike our own have to consider two factors which, while not peculiar to us, are peculiar to those traveling with a message: (1) we cannot communicate our message without using the tools of culture, and (2) it is very likely that our message will alter some expressions of the culture we are working in, perhaps significantly.

We cannot master the technicalities of the first of these factors unless we are settled in our minds that we are indeed willing to undertake the second, that is, unless we are willing to accept such alterations of culture as the gospel will require. Many cultural scientists (included in this category are artisans both in social sciences and ethnic studies) are unwilling to allow any alteration of culture, especially an unstudied culture. They sometimes seem to be saying that culture is itself the good: culture reflects the human condition and only by knowing all we can know about all cultures will we know all the possible human potentialities and activities. Such a position will conserve some of the glories of humanness, but it ignores moral judgments. The human situation is itself the value (to them). Sin, in this framework, is a concept peculiar to those cultures accepting the standards of a god or gods. There may exist concepts of social wrong, scientific error, or violations of clan codes, but these reflect mores deriving from the accident of climate or tribal rivalry or simply the stronger personalities of the culture. It would be almost axiomatic that there are no overarching standards judging culture itself. The mores of one culture cannot be fully meaningful or translatable in another.

Christians agree in principle that most cultures should not impose their values on a different culture, but they approach culture from a radically different starting point in two important aspects. First, Christians believe that all persons were created for fellowship with God. This divine-human dialogue can only be expressed in the tools of human culture—at least some of the tools. Much of culture is inevitably neutral, potentially expressing either rejection of God or

Indigenous Music 117

intimate love and fellowship with Him. Culture is not a value in itself but a tool. It is God who is good; His expression of Himself is good. Persons as God created them to be are good, and culture is good only as it expresses that creation in its original intent.

Second, human beings are fallen. They are fallen not simply because they violated the mores of their tribe (although that may happen to be a sin), nor because they overindulged (again, they might have known better), nor because they accidentally broke an arbitrary rule (God's rules are never arbitrary from the standpoint of His perfect nature.) but because they rejected fellowship with God. This is the primary sin, and secondary sin, sin against one's fellow, is wrong because it repudiates God's larger plan for mutuality. Culture is a picture of the human condition; it reflects what people are, and much of that is disastrous.

Christianity is not a phenomenon of culture. It has found expression in radically different ages, climates, cultures, and languages.

Can Christ be expressed in only one cultural mold?

> This would be tantamount to saying that he could only be expressed in one language. The genius of first-century Christianity lay in its plastic adaptability to a wide variety of expressions. The Christian faith cannot be fully understood without its Hebrew roots, yet it spread quickly to Greek expressions both in North Africa and Asia Minor, and on to Latin expressions—within the century. The Reformation brought a renascence with very distinctive patterns in the German Lutheran, French-Swiss Reformed, and English church models. The twentieth-century church is debtor to a multifaceted, culturally diverse complex of traditions. Would God suddenly freeze his pattern of the use of culture as the missionary movement expands? God is obviously not responsible for every event of history, but he is the God of history. From the beginning, God used culture, and it has been the pattern of Christianity to flow easily into new containers over and over again.[3]

It is probably a safe assumption that Christianity has successfully penetrated and survived in a wider variety of life-styles and cultures

118   Music in Missions: Discipling Through Music

than any other religion on earth; indeed, today it maintains survival in radically different cultures. Oriental religions have found their way into the West and Islam is worldwide, but they have not yet impacted generations *in cultures radically different from that of their origins* in the same way that Christianity has done throughout the centuries. Christianity established long ago that it does not need culture for survival but for communication, vertically with God and horizontally with persons.

And how has it achieved that? I venture the premise that *it survives precisely because it is acultural and its demand is otherworldliness.* It does not despise culture, nor does it worship culture. Its end is not culture but Christ. If our worship of Him is the end and purpose of redemption, then any tool that does not conflict with holiness may be used in His worship and His business, but the tool is secondary. If Christianity does indeed demand "otherworldliness" (perhaps not its primary orientation in the minds of some twentieth-century Christians, but see 2 Peter 1:4, 1 John 2:15-17, and so forth), then culture is an opportunity or a problem only as it somehow opens doors for expression of that which is supremely acultural, a spiritual world superior to and far more important than the culture that allows it expression.

An "otherworldly" view of Christianity no more denigrates culture than it denigrates the body. The body, if we believe the first chapters of Genesis, is good; all that God meant humanity to be is good. The body speaks eloquently of the genius of the divine creation, and Christianity maintains that there will be a "spiritual body." In the same way, culture also reveals aspects of humanness that glorify God, perhaps more than the most eloquent sermon.[4] It even seems likely that less-sophisticated cultures contain elements of the glory of humanness long spoiled by more "advanced" societies. So culture is at once our greatest opportunity and our most stubborn problem. Few things reveal more of the divine genius and human nobility; nothing else demonstrates more painfully the dreadful distance humans have interposed between themselves and the Creator of all good. Because of this, missionaries approach their problems

Indigenous Music   119

with a profound respect for culture, but they believe that culture itself is not the highest good. Their primary intention is not to preserve culture but to preach Christ.

A missionary's very calling is to universals which are fixed and inviolable, but he or she communicates through a culture which is subject to change. The message (Christ) and its implications (the demands implicit in God's nature with its demand for new standards governing vertical and horizontal relationships) cannot be compromised. Culture on the other hand is not an absolute, however valuable it might be. Most cultures experience various degrees of continuous change, and in the twentieth century, change is almost inevitable. Missionaries find themselves willy-nilly forced to participate in the process of change by virtue of their office.[5] They must seek neither to westernize nor to avoid the demands of life in Christ. Theirs is the dreadfully serious problem of assisting and guiding new converts through an understanding of the nature of their new Christian experience, with all the changes which newness implies for them as Christ lives out His life in the converts' culture.

Musical Style

We have discussed culture in general, but what about musical styles? What about the close connection music has in many cultures with dance, storytelling, poetry, tribal history, and so forth? These two questions are closely related because on them the very definition of music hangs. Music in most of Africa south of the Sahara is simply not music without the involvement of the body. We are grateful that the Bible answers this question, at least. Both Miriam (Ex. 15:20) and David (2 Sam. 6:16) danced before the Lord.

One of the most thrilling and versatile cultural forms in Indonesia is the folk dance. We should somehow develop this form to tell the story of Jesus and to glorify God, even as David did. Many Indonesians look on the Western dance as sexually degrading, but they can become completely absorbed in their folk dances because these are true cultural forms, and not immorally suggestive.[6]

The uses of music in the Bible are staggering in their rich diversity. Music was used with the dance for storytelling, drama, anointing, playing, harvesting, general rejoicing, and worship—and we have only begun to name its uses.

Style is a more complex question, but there can be no question that the Bible does not touch on the matter of style (or of taste for that matter). The Bible accepts purely instrumental music, purely vocal music, and unimagined combinations of the two. The fact is that so many styles have found acceptance in the church during her two-thousand-year history that history cannot be a criterion. We are left with common sense and our sense of propriety guided by the Holy Spirit to discern which styles are acceptable to the Lord, and actually do serve as vehicles to worship Him with. But our common sense would be grossly offended if we could hear the music of many of the Bible cultures or of the church in history. We are likely to be less flexible in the matter of style than in any other musical matter. Spreading the gospel through music requires more humility than most of us can imagine.

The real issue lies in what a given culture understands as music. Music may consist of gutteral grunts, of the sound coming from the friction of rubbing every sort of material together, of a combination of several folk arts such as dancing or drama, of rhythmic sounds without any melody as we understand it, of melodies with only one or two notes, of pitches and tunings incomprehensible to an average Western ear—in short, of materials and activities almost entirely outside the experience of an average European. But the same thing could almost certainly be said of some of the music of Bible times. We would not call it music.

Indigenous Music

Principles

With these factors in mind, the advice of many experienced missionaries might be summed up in a few general principles:

1. *Everything good in a culture should be retained.* The fact that a cultural expression may seem radically different need not rouse suspicion. Our primary concern should be about relationships, both with God and with people. Remember that the Bible sanctions festivity in harvesting, getting married, birthing babies, and in all of life. The missionary should assume that God has provided more than adequate resources for picturing Himself in the culture of the people he is working with.

2. *Everything obviously and inherently evil should be discarded.* Again we run into a problem. Snake dances involving demon worship and the like are out of the question for believers. There also may be a pattern of certain musical styles being reserved for these kinds of activities, but musical styles change. The pub song picked up by William Fry in the late nineteenth century and set to the words "I have found a Friend in Jesus" has no ring of its origin today. Still, the future is not the missionary's problem as he guides his converts. His concern is simply that the music in church not remind the believers of their own former attachment to the pagan or to sinful habits, at least not to the extent of arousal.

3. *One may trust the Holy Spirit in the gray areas, especially as He guides a new believer if that believer is being carefully discipled.* Most missionaries report that it is the believers themselves who are strictest in interpreting their new life. But caution is a very good light if it does not make us fearful or prevent us from appreciating the good in the culture.

4. *Missionaries should carefully and prayerfully evaluate how much of their message and how many of their standards are biblical and universal and which are conditioned by their own cultural background.* In general these standards may include such things as hair styles, preferences for a specific number of weekly church meetings, or a preference for a particular extrabiblical pattern of church organizations. Musically, it includes the uncon-

122   Music in Missions: Discipling Through Music

scious prejudice that a certain melodic, harmonic, or rhythmic idiom or style expresses specific ethos in one's experience of God.

It is extremely difficult, for example, for a Westerner to grasp what meaning an African reads into his rhythm. Western rhythmic styles are extremely monotonous, droning endlessly in a metric sequence established at the beginning of a song and never abandoned until the end of the song. Rhythm usually, at least in hymnody, provides background for the real meaning attended to in the melody or harmony. It is there to maintain a constant grid behind the variations of tonal materials. Westerners, if they think of rhythm at all, tend to classify the metric constant as neutral at best, or potentially evil at worst. But in sub-Sahara Africa, rhythm tends to be a fascinating and constant variation of time materials, unbelievably complex, and patterned in shifting and variegated time ideas entirely outside the experience and understanding of anyone not conditioned and trained by long experience in it. Meters change; various drummers enter with strong beats on another drummer's weak beats; phrases are repeated, interjected, and varied at seemingly unpredictable will; a vital and energetic drummer's dialogue interchanges ideas completely foreign to the experience of outsiders. In short, nothing in the Western missionary's background prepares him or her to understand that meaning in African music is inextricably bound to rhythm, and to know what that meaning is.

So missionaries not only must help nationals sift through the relation of culture to their lives in Christ, they must also release their own expressions of Christianity which are extra-biblical. At the same time they must cling to that which is unmistakably universal and valid.

5. *The missionary should regard the tools of culture as an important means of communication, second only to language.* Indeed, one cannot know language apart from culture. This does not always mean that a nonmusician should learn the technicalities of the new music system, but surely one would want to know what it *sounds* like, at least enough to identify differences in the major dialects of a given musical language

Indigenous Music   **123**

and to appreciate their significance in society—just as in American music (admittedly rich in subcultures), one can distinguish between jazz and folk song or between rock and a hymn or between country and an art song.

The music specialist, of course, will want to acquire as many tools of ethnomusicology as possible.[7] The purpose is to encourage and develop the national leadership, not to be a leader oneself. It would seem that music specialists would feel more compulsion than other missionaries to seek to win the musical leadership of a village or nation since they are probably more aware of the need of the body of Christ for musical resources for worship. Since they will function as guides, they should master as much of the local vocabulary of music as possible. Missionaries who have mastered the indigenous musical styles report enthusiastic reception of their efforts to make music with the nationals.[8]

If missionaries do succeed in mastering the local style so that they are somewhat accepted by nationals as they perform in their style, what can they do with their new skills? It is important first to recognize what they will normally *not* do. Normally, they will not attempt to teach nationals in their own styles. They will not teach music, and they will not teach songs (although they will be very likely to teach theory or notation). When Gerald Workman was working in northern Malawi in the early 1970s, he found that:

> The best teaching technique for helping people learn new songs is:
> 1. Use of the tape recorder with an African group performing. The recording should be used as a demonstration and not as singalong. In teaching the song, the teacher should be an African.
> 2. The other way is for an African who knows the song to [sing and] teach it to the people.[9]

The missionary will not lead music. The presence or absence of the missionary in corporate worship should be a minor factor from the first; the functioning of the church body should not depend on that. Missionaries may be a part of the nationals' interaction with the

124　　　　　　Music in Missions: Discipling Through Music

Lord, but if they are the only or even the main reason for that interaction, worship will cease as soon as they disappear from the scene. They are there to plant Christ, not themselves.[10] If they led the music, it would likely be unidiomatic, and yet their prestige would incline the members to believe that their style is more "Christian" than that of the national. They can, in fact, measure the success of their work by the quality of worship which goes on in their absence; if it continues on an even keel whenever they are away, they have some assurance that it would do so if they were removed permanently.

Normally, they will not perform on a regular basis whenever local talent is available. Performance (such as a musical solo) may be justified on two bases: (1) The soloist may present a message from the Lord—an appeal or an exhortation; one will be in dialogue with the congregation if one's music is a message. (2) One may represent the congregation in their worshipful address to God; the dialogue in this case is with God, alongside the congregation as their spokesman. If the missionary is performing the first of these functions, as soloist he or she is endangering another concept—that the natural and spiritual gifts of every believer, including nationals, are useful to the body of Christ. Sometimes nationals are reluctant to perform if the missionary has been seen as a performer although it is also possible in some situations that the missionary's performance serves as a model to imitate. If the missionary is performing the second function, one is in danger of being seen in a priestly role rather than that of spokesman. One other factor is that missionaries who sing solos often choose Western music and styles with which they are more comfortable. This might be acceptable in an area with much musical syncretism; in a pioneer area it would likely state that their choice of music is more "Christian."

The degree of avoidance of these three activities—teaching, leading, performing—will vary considerably according to the needs of a specific field. In much of sub-Sahara Africa, they would be avoided altogether; in Latin America there is more room for them because its

Indigenous Music 125

culture approximates North American more closely. However, even when the culture is in styles more closely approximating Western styles, we must still realize that there are really two dangers—a violation of cultural style and a violation of mission method. The missionary may have mastered the style, but the desire is still that the work of the national church be done by national Christians. The decision to do any of the three will require sensitivity and insight. Generally, one will have a hierarchy of avoidance: one is least likely to teach national styles, somewhat more likely to lead music in worship if occasion arises, and one will feel more freedom to perform than to teach or lead.

So what can the missionary do positively that will help and encourage local Christians? The following six activities are suggestive and not exhaustive.

1. One may encourage nationals that their music is acceptable, their spiritual gifts valid, and their talents valuable to God and to the church. If the work is in a pioneer area, the missionary knows more about the workings of Christianity and the teachings of the Bible than anyone else. His opinion is usually more highly respected.

2. One may use one's leverage to encourage the use of biblical principles. Texts should be faithful to the spirit of Scripture. The high calling of spiritual worship should be a priority. God, not mankind or self, should be elevated.

3. One may participate in congregational worship. One's attitudes toward God through worship will be communicated whether they are sound or not. One should, of course, avoid being so conspicuous that all eyes will fall on oneself.

4. One will usually do well to assist nationals in getting their own music into some form of notation. The First International Conference of Baptist Church Musicians (for East Africa only) in Blantyre, Malawi, in March of 1978 debated this issue at some length. There was concern that if nationals started "freezing" their music in notation their natural and delightful skills in improvisation might deteriorate. The second such conference (including all Africa) in November of

1981, unlike the first, enjoyed the presence and contributions of several gifted national musicians. It was the nationals who led the missionaries to position themselves in favor of teaching Western staff notation to nationals.

There were a number of reasons for this position: it would expand considerably the dissemination of new music; it would give the nationals more musical "tools" to think with; it would preserve much music which at present is ephemeral and yet deserves preservation; and it would facilitate the process of learning new music. Other notational systems were not discussed because it was felt that none had established itself sufficiently to be generally useful, and many nationals were already somewhat familiar with staff notation. Tonic sol-fa notation was considered too cumbersome for the sophisticated rhythms of most drummers. Missionaries who had observed the rapid dissemination of new songs and who had seen choirs learn four-part harmony and even polyphony with astonishing speed by rote questioned the validity of the need for any kind of notation, but the nationals prevailed. In that conference, at least, the nationals were extremely anxious to learn how to write their songs down.

5. One can provide numberless helps behind the scenes. Various kinds of promotional activities provide fellowship and stimulation of indigenous music: festivals, encouragement of choirs or programs, journals of church music or informal interchanges of ideas in any form,[11] and publication of the efforts of national composers, however crude the form and the physical layout may be. Here is one of the areas of expertise which need not necessarily threaten the initial roles of national musicians, although the missionary will be prepared to step back as soon as development allows a national to step into the promotional role also.

6. One can seek out, encourage, and develop national talent. What kind of talent? Primarily local church leaders but also composers, singers, instrumentalists, hymn writers, and so forth.

Missionaries working with previously unreached peoples have the potential of developing a church music which is natural and yet

Indigenous Music 127

sacred in style, of allowing the growth of worship which is sincere, untainted by prejudice, commercialism, or sophistication, and of helping preserve the best of culture while bringing it under the lordship of Christ. It is an unusually thrilling challenge, a historic opportunity, and a weighty responsibility.

Syncretistic Areas

Very few areas of the world are untouched by other cultures. In a day of widespread radio and cassette usage, even rural sections of undeveloped areas will be familiar with many kinds of music. Tribal peoples in much of Africa speak several tribal languages and often one or two trade languages. It is likely that missionaries can have access to a certain amount of literature on the musics of these more developed areas, and, therefore, they are less likely to need investigative techniques as such, although of course a modest acquaintance with ethnomusicology will give one insights that cannot be gained any other way.

The most effective musical language will always be the first language of the local group, even though they may be familiar with other styles. It is the ability of the nationals to use other styles which has occasioned such controversy at times in the world of missions.[12] Some missiologists insist on demanding only the original local styles; others are more lenient. It would seem that a cautious and reverent respect for the ability of the nationals to discern the leadership of the Holy Spirit should characterize missionaries in this situation. Missionaries can offer guidance, but openness and humility should allow the nationals the ultimate decisions as to what music they will sing.

Nevertheless, missionary guidance is crucial, and they are there to help them avoid pitfalls into which their inexperience might lead. Certain factors must be considered and occasionally pointed out; these are best combined with an understanding of the more urban areas. Developing areas are on their way to becoming urban.

Urban Areas

An outstanding language teacher once said that one can be fluent in another language without being bilingual. She illustrated this by saying that persons truly bilingual in English and another language would Anglicize the words (such as proper nouns) of their other language if they were speaking English. Those merely fluent in a language will insist on the "foreign" pronunciation of foreign names, even while speaking English. In urban areas, there will be found persons who are "fluent" in several musical languages but are not actually bi-musical. This is undoubtedly true anywhere in the world. Few prejudices are as strong as our musical ones. An area may appear to be quite urbane or catholic in its variety of musical expressions, yet the people may be strongly inclined to express their deepest feelings in one particular musical style.

The only satisfactory answer is that the missionary's first desire is to communicate. It is probably true that one will find handles for communicating to people-*groups* more easily in pioneer and syncretistic areas, but in urban areas one will find it harder to discover common interests for groups, so they will need to be more sensitive on the level of the *individual*, that is, to persons. In urban areas, there will be nationals who prefer the musical language of their childhood home and others who prefer national styles because of the influence of nationalism. There may also be some who will prefer Western styles because of a desire for "progress;" yet others will prefer Western music because they are truly more familiar with it. If it is possible for one to discover the motivation behind preferences, one may be able to speak to their unrevealed but genuine inclinations.

What the missionary must discover is simply what is *life* to the nationals, where they are most likely to express intimacy. What language do they pray in? They may prefer for a stately hymn to be in a Western style in English or a trade language, but in what language do they prefer to do their personal Bible study? What music do they sing in the kitchen or at leisure? They may prefer the study

Indigenous Music   129

of Western music, but what would they play on the record player in their most relaxed moments?

If the missionaries cannot reach all of the people with a single musical style, they surely will seek to reach as many as possible and to disciple them with the tools at hand, even if it requires a multifaceted fluency in several musical styles. Urban areas will hold more tolerant attitudes. Older Christians can be taught generosity in accepting the whims of new Christians.

It could well be argued that catholicity is an ultimate ideal for any assembly of real disciples, especially in urban areas. The Jerusalem church was certainly quite diverse in the various cultural groups participating. What bound them was not culture but an exciting new faith in Christ. That pattern continued throughout the New Testament period; the churches were mixtures of Jews and Gentiles, nationals and foreigners. Paul, a Jewish Pharisee, quoted hymns in Greek. The great urban centers—Rome, Corinth, and so forth—must have had churches quite diverse in makeup. And is this, after all, not an important part of what constitutes the good news? Christ erases barriers; He does not reinforce them. In Him, the knowledge of God supersedes the glories of humanness.

Thus music will serve different functions in different cultures. In some cultures, it will serve as a primary vehicle for *reaching* the unreached. In these cases, the music must be that which will be understood by them and cannot be catholic. In other cultures, we will need a more catholic pattern to reach a variety of people. Ultimately, music will serve the broader purposes of discipleship, and catholicity might reflect a more developed and mature outlook.

In urban areas, it is possible to expose Christians to the classics of the church.[13] Evidently, we would have to distinguish between "classical" (universal) and "traditional" (local or national). The classical, presumably, would provide exposure to a very wide variety of experience: chorales, gospel hymns, Victorian hymns, Latin and Greek hymns, and so forth. In most hymnals of highly developed countries, regardless of the degree of Christianization, there probably could be

Music in Missions: Discipling Through Music

found a group of universally accepted classics. No doubt it could be established that the various classical styles reflect the needs or propensities of specific cultures, but their very universality proves at least something of their validity for all Christians. As the church has expanded, the pattern has always been that time (if not maturity) brings an expansion of the musical literature of the body. It is extremely likely that the pattern has been: for evangelism, find the most "immediate," locally viable and suitable music possible; for discipleship, worship, and nurture, expand the horizons of the believers.

Notes

1. G. William Supplee, "Principles of Incorporating Music of Other Cultures in the Music of the Church," paper presented to the National Church Music Fellowship Convention, Grand Rapids, Mich., 1971, pp. 1-4.

2. The the term *pioneer* rather than "rural" is chosen because many quite rural peoples are in fact syncretistic. The terms *pioneer, syncretistic,* and *urban* attempt to describe something of the mind-set which the missionary attempting to communicate with the target group must understand.

3. T. W. Hunt, "Witnessing through Culture," Chapter 11 of *Educating for Christian Missions,* ed. Arthur L. Walker, Jr. (Nashville, Broadman Press, 1981), p. 143.

4. Vida Chenoweth states this very charmingly in *The Usarufas and Their Music,* SIL Museum of Anthropology, Dallas, 1979, p. xv: "Some of us believe that every language and every music is needed to adequately reflect the Creator of man."

5. The problem may be unspeakably more complex than surface appearances indicate. With the help of the Holy Spirit, the missionary will probably find little difficulty in convincing a convert of the hostility to Christianity in practices, say, such as human sacrifice or ritual dismembering of bodies. The various ramifications of initiation rites or even wedding ceremonies will be considerably more problematic.

6. Unsigned questionnaire, January-March, 1967. The objection to social dancing in many evangelical circles has more than cultural grounds. By the term *dance* is generally understood couple dancing, and the specific associations with sexual suggestion and lust appall many sensitive Christians. On the other hand, evangelicals limit their witness by a refusal to see the cultural aspects of the problem in mission work. Culture may train us toward guilt or innocence in any activity.

7. Missionaries already on the field without a background in investigative procedure may begin their exploration of this vast and useful field with such works as: Bruno Nettle, *Theory and Method in Ethnomusicology,* The Free Press of Glencoe, 1964 (especially pp. 73-85); Alan P. Merriam, *The Anthropology of Music,* Evanston, Northwest-

Indigenous Music 131

ern University Press, 1964; and Vida Chenoweth, *Melodic Perception and Analysis: A Manual on Ethnic Melody*, Ukarumpa, Papua, New Guinea, Summer Institute of Linguistics, 1973. These will provide very different aspects of the approaches and have the advantage of combining technical procedures with cultural orientation early in the development of technique. *Missiology, An International Review* brings evangelical mission purpose to occasional studies on ethnic hymnody, and *Ethnomusicology* (journal for the Society for Ethnomusicology) provides continuing models of research, as well as help missionaries keep abreast of the development of refinements in method. These volumes and periodicals will also help them locate the available literature on their geographical areas as well as an extensive bibliography on the various concerns of ethnological understanding and mission method. Obviously, it is impossible for most missionaries to achieve professional competence in such highly specialized disciplines as ethnomusicology just as they cannot in all the specialized areas of theology. But they can obtain insights, develop skills, and widen mission endeavor in areas too often ignored by Christian missionaries in the past.

8. For example, Rennie Ohtani in Tokyo, who is considered an expert on the koto.

9. Letter to the author, 8 Jan. 1973.

10. The author is aware of the axiom that the missionary does not "take Christ to Africa" (or wherever); Christ is already there. But isn't this to avoid the issue? If one is a missionary, one does not "take Christ to Africa," one introduces Him to *people*, and these people may happen to be Africans or Texans. It is spreading the rule of Christ in the hearts of persons that motivates a divinely called missionary.

11. Nathan Corbitt in Kenya has an outstanding journal, *The Kenyan Musician*, mimeographed, which has been very encouraging to gifted church musicians there.

12. See, for example, Elaine T. Lewis, James M. Riccitelli, and William L. Smalley, "More about Developing Non-Western Hymnody," *Practical Anthropology*, Jan.-Feb. 1964, pp. 35-46.

13. The 1980 Africa Music Conference was somewhat hesitant about defining one corpus as universally "classical."

7

Indigenization

The dictionary provides as an antonymn of *indigenous, naturalized.*[1] The missionary, however, will usually be working with such a variety of musics that often even nationals themselves may not be sure which styles are native to a given area. In some areas (for example, much of southeast Asia, much of Africa south of the Sahara), sharply distinguished styles may survive in a form almost totally untouched by the outside world. In others, local styles may survive while the local people know and appreciate other subcultures within their nation. The stately Sardana of Catalonia in northeastern Spain is quite unrelated to the impetuous Flamenco of Andalusia in the south (and this is true to some extent of all the musics of Spain), and yet Catalonian people have a certain "big-brother" fondness for the Andalusian styles, understand them, and often have a certain fluency in performing them (although regional loyalties and rivalries are fierce). Add to this the fact that Catalonians retain a propensity for the German chorale while Andalusians, often at least, prefer the gospel song: one, old European and the other clearly nineteenth-century American (but neither really Spanish). In the face of a bewildering array of choices, can an outsider even make suggestions?

Problems

Whatever the situation, effective methodology should be directed toward church growth, with all that that implies. The factors discussed here will prevail anytime we talk about a cultural situation.

Indigenization 133

Again, the seven problems discussed below are somewhat arbitrary in their delimitation, but any discussion of mission methodology should be suggestive rather than definitive, regardless.

1. *The effectiveness of the medium chosen is primary, and is best determined locally by sensitive and experienced nationals and missionaries together, where that is possible.* Choice of communicative media should be on the basis of their comprehensibility, meaning, suggestiveness, and function within their environment for the national. A communicative vehicle must relate to life as the target audience has known it; it must have vitality. The day is long past when vitality can be measured by traditional Occidental concepts. The association of minor keys with sadness, for example, characterizes a relatively small segment of Western history. Donald Hustad has stated, "Our missionaries—our pastors and evangelists too—will have to give up that telling point in their sermons: that music of the natives was all in the minor key until they heard the gospel."[2]

2. *Both taste and meaning are conditioned by past associations.* The most stubborn musical associations often result from the mission history itself, especially where a given work is older. Earlier missionaries sometimes taught, either deliberately or unconsciously, that indigenous music was heathen, and contemporary believers are heirs to prejudices so strong that it seems unwise to force changes too rapidly. Where communication might be enhanced by change, the problem is especially difficult because even though new believers might be attracted more by a purer indigeneity, the very ones who will be their most effective disciplers are the ones who are resisting change. Elaine Lewis explained that one cannot assume that one is working in a vacuum.

> We have encouraged Christians to produce songs to be used in evangelistic work that are written in the style of native music, and in which the tunes match the tones . . . but it has not caught on as we had hoped . . .
>
> However, in an area such as Burma, where the Christian church has

existed for nearly 150 years, we find that it is not . . . simple. We must begin where the people are. We must let the national Christians make the decisions as to what kind of music they will use in their churches, and then fit into the situation as gracefully as we can.[3]

James Riccitelli cautioned, "But in such areas, has Christianity succeeded in *changing* the culture, or simply imposing a layer of veneer?"[4] Still, the veneer is at times a valid product of acculturation, which possibility Riccitelli acknowledged. Brazilian nationals, for example, have almost always reported a strong preference for the gospel song over indigenous forms; even believers from an Oriental culture such as Cantonese Hong Kong have stoutly defended the naturalness to literate Chinese of Western church music. At the same time, the indigenous idiom is likely to remain as a *characteristic* expression of the culture. Even when nationals become so acculturated as to prefer North American or European styles (as, say, in the countries of the Orient which have a high culture in their history) the possibility of a latent loyalty to the older remains a factor in the shifting tides of nationalism.

Persistence of the local musical language indicates its viability as a communicative vehicle.

Most tribal peoples of the world are in some degree of a transition stage now. But changes come slowly. In many cases musical habits remain with a people even after other cultural changes have been made . . . Some thread of continuity holds people together when former folkways are being replaced or destroyed. Since musical style is often one of these threads of continuity, is it not reasonable to use it rather than destroy it too?[5]

William Smalley pointed out a significant aspect of the problem:

In the situation which Mrs. Lewis describes I suspect that Western music has become a form so closely identified with the church that the development of an indigenous hymnody has become difficult not on musical grounds but on "theological." Western culture (i.e., hymn tunes) is so closely identified with Christianity that anything else is

Indigenization   135

non-Christian. This, of course, is theological heresy, and is culturally stultifying. I feel we have a responsibility to lead or stimulate local people in the development of their cultural heritage in the church, not to the exclusion of Western music, but to the enrichment of the whole musical life and an appeal to a wider range of people.[6]

Certainly, to miss that which newer Christians might say to us through their culture would be irreparable loss, and at the same time it would seem disastrous to ignore a well-established heritage. As Riccitelli admited, "Patterns, good and bad, are established and any break in the pattern is always strongly resisted."[7] Both, in fact, are needed. The introduction of indigenous hymns and hymn tunes is not only feasible but needful in most mission situations, and the wider experience of heritage is valuable. No pat answer will be universally applicable; a cultivated sensitivity to the possibilities is urgently needed.

A second problem of musical association is that in which indigenous music bears strongly unchristian connotations. Here again we must discern those prejudices which reflect native assessment of the actual situation and those resulting from the teaching of former missionaries that the indigenous is heathen. An extraordinary study by Delbert Rice may serve as a model for filtering the various facets through a fine theological-ethnological screen. In a thorough investigation of music categories as patterned by the iKalahan of the Philippines, he listed the various cultural settings for music, and the types of song utilized in each. Bases for acceptance or rejection of various forms were: (1) The *angba* was "an esoteric music limited to certain occasions which do not correspond to a fellowship meeting of Christians" and was "inextricably associated with a *religious* ceremony which is, by its very nature, non-Christian." (2) The humorous *dayomti* "could only be used if the contents of the poem were definitely humorous," such as Christ's injunction to remove the log from one's eye before attempting to clean dust from a neighbor's. (3) The reverie *dayomti* was a usable vehicle because it was used "to express deep

136   Music in Missions: Discipling Through Music

emotion and also to influence moral or spiritual behavior through symbolic or semisymbolic interpretation." (4) The heart call *dayomti* could be appropriate in prayers for forgiveness or a funeral. (5) The *gomigom* was too brief for normal congregational singing but might be employed for short forms such as proverbs. (6) The *ba-liw,* being extemporaneous, could be adapted for dialogue or dramatic presentations but, obviously, could not be employed for unison singing.[8]

3. *Extraneous factors should not intrude.* The most obvious of these is personal taste, which is no doubt the most difficult to assess and evaluate honestly. Missionaries should begin their assessment with a determination not to be unrealistic—to face their own prejudices. We might start by examining some of the expressions that we use to describe our own various musical experiences such as *beautiful, catchy,* and so forth. *Catchy* cannot even translate in some European languages with a one-word equivalent, and certainly not in many non-European languages. The problem is not merely linguistic but experiential. The idea *catchy* is not a part of the experience of some cultures.

Another extraneous factor is the question of the historical identity of Christianity with Western culture. Because of this, many nationals prefer complete separation from their "heathen" heritage. The opposite is the national who accepts Christ but is identified with a national rejection of Western culture or a tide of rising allegiance to native forms, especially in high cultures. Ideally, the identification of Christianity with certain cultural forms would be identified and labeled for just what it is—an *extraneous* factor. This would seem to be primarily a matter of theological understanding, correctible through explanation, and acceptance of higher levels of evaluation by both missionary and national. But prejudice runs strong, and this question will require considerable prayer and thought.

4. *Words and music will relate differently in different cultures.* The first point at which the missionary touches this problem is in translation. The text obviously should be comprehensible in terms of local world view and custom. Certain poetic devices are peculiar to the English language and are rarely translatable. Attempts at rendering the original

Indigenization

English idea may present an actual inaccuracy in literal translation because of the linguistic pattern of expressing imagery ("golden dreams" becomes "dreams of gold" in some languages). Many figures are geographical in origin and are meaningless in cultures where latitude does not allow expression of the original idea—allusions to winter or to snow in equatorial areas; the use of *white* to describe purity; the use of harvest crops in areas where these same crops are not grown or where some local crop would be more effective; such terms as *moor and fen, pavilioned in splendor,* and so forth.

Tonal languages present an extremely difficult problem. Although a few tonal languages apparently do not always require exact musical correspondence for comprehensibility, it is well established that lack of correspondence is a positive barrier to an understanding of the text by the uninitiated.[9] The full ramifications of this difficulty are only beginning to be understood. It will probably dictate that each new stanza of a given hymn will require a different musical setting, that is, it will be strophic in its composition unless the poet manages to adjust the *text* to match tone.

Riccitelli suggested balancing such a quantity of change by frequent interpolation of refrains, that is, repeating the same words with the same music often.[10] I have encountered Christian nationals who do not object to a lack of tone-tune correspondence even when the uninitiated fail to understand the words; one national stated that "most educated people will get it." But if the *uninitiated* cannot understand, it is the duty of the missionary to lead and encourage (however gently) in the development of a truly indigenous hymnody which demonstrates the ability to communicate at least the text, regardless of prior experience in the vocabulary of the Christian experience. Riccitelli suggested a twelve-point guide in developing a hymnody:

1. The music is a vehicle to carry the words; the words are ultimately more important than the music, for it is the words that will edify.
2. What are the differences in the fundamentals of music of the

missionary's native language and the language in which he wishes to develop a hymnody?

3. Pay attention to accent in the music and in the words.
4. What about slurs in the music?
5. Note the pauses or "breaks" or semipauses in the music.
6. Watch out for diphthongs.
7. Do syllables exist that are almost "swallowed" and apparently don't need a full note?
8. Does tone exist in the language?
9. Never force grammar.
10. Give attention to subject matter.
11. Are certain time signatures preferred [in native tunes]?
12. What is the native poetry?[11]

Rhythmic, accentual, and metrical problems are also explored by Riccitelli, Chenoweth, Key, and Rice in their studies. These include such complex questions as the relation of vowel length to note value, the acceptable margin of violation of language rhythm, the problem of languages which tend to avoid accents and long vowels, and poetic meter.

Perhaps two basic guides will sum up the philosophy missionaries should bring to all their efforts in adapting music to words: (1) comprehensibility is the prime aim, and (2) a given setting of a musical text should be pleasing to the national ear. Too often the national will accept a setting that expresses the idea (Conventional politeness is often a barrier in procuring a valid assessment.) when a more idiomatic way is possible. It is very important to seek ways of tapping the resources of the national's more sensitive ear, even if it means finding a non-Christian informant.

5. *Missionaries must identify and articulate the conscious and unconscious standards of their upbringing and separate them from those of the missionary purpose.* Few agencies will appoint missionaries whose history exhibits cultural or racial prejudicies, and yet Christly ministers of all sorts are subject to unconscious influences from their home and native environments. Missionaries have occasionally been shocked to find that

Indigenization

139

they have offended with a term like "native." Too often, musical standards are (often unconsciously) fixed with reference to a supposed inferiority, or primitiveness of a culture. This is not to deny the existence of cultural levels; certainly, it is not to deny the enormous variations that exist between literate and nonliterate cultures. Within any culture there are levels (easily seen in North American culture), and it would be unrealistic to ignore them.

Christly missionaries simply begin from a different point of view—that of Jesus Christ. They begin where the people are. Their vocabulary expresses a love which is indifferent to station, the outstretched and longing arms of an inviting God, the expression of Christ within culture, and the permeating, filling, blessing of the Holy Spirit in (perhaps hitherto unsuspected) avenues of human expression. Their point of departure is, in a word, communication, rather than standards.

6. *Missionary must retrain their hearing by a new kind of listening.* We hear in terms of our past associations. Western ears often cannot hear pitch and rhythmic subtleties in many non-Western scales or modes. Nationals, on the other hand, sometimes do not hear diatonic progressions if accustomed to pentatonic or hexatonic scales. If adjustment is to be made at all, it must begin with the missionary. Both the national and the missionary can grow in hearing perception of unfamiliar intervals, if their point of departure is not a standards problem. When missionaries complain that the national cannot sing in tune, they are often indicating their own lack of sensitivity to the consistency of the national scale tuning. That growth is possible and feasible is demonstrated by the fact that Western ears grow in perception of fine tuning of Western music itself, with musical training.

7. *The missionary must be practical.* In many climates, the kulintang, calabash, or even accordion or guitar, are more practical than pianos and organs. Portability must be considered if mobility is at all desirable. Another aspect of practicality is the teachability of much Western music; tonal patterns may be too difficult to absorb. Economics is still another factor: the smaller the instrument, the smaller the

140　　　　　　　Music in Missions: Discipling Through Music

hymnbook, the simpler the apparatus, the more likely the national or the church will be able to afford it or to build it or to make it.

Indigenization—Procedures

Encouragement and Development of the National

Throughout the discussion of these seven problem areas, it should be increasingly evident that most of the time, the national worker in music, if one is available, would already possess all those attributes for solution of the problem and application of practical solutions that the missionary so wishes to develop. The national performs the music idiomatically; he is not hampered by preconceived or unconscious standards of North American taste; he instinctively applies words to music according to indigenous idioms; he has no hearing problem with reference to intervals; he possibly plays those native instruments most likely to be accepted in Christian worship.

Missionary strategy, therefore, will from the beginning aim toward *discovery* of musical talent, *evangelization and enlistment* of music workers, and *training* of them.

Discovery. Musical anthropologists have already begun to place considerable information at our disposal concerning the finding of local musicians. Where musical leadership does not surface immediately (the ideal situation), or where the missionary is seeking to enlarge the quantity of workers available, the social mores of a given culture will provide helpful clues in the search for talent. Present evidence seems to indicate that specialization in music is usually practiced in non-Western cultures,[12] but from the standpoint of missionaries seeking the development of church leaders for church growth, it is possible theoretically that tribal musicians may be designated by the community or by tradition or family lineage: the assignment may be a social or traditional function on bases other than talent. In actual practice, since music leaders emerge from converts, the problem of discovery is helped by the action of the Holy Spirit. Obviously, the missionary wishes to evangelize those musically talented, and will, in the process

Indigenization   141

of his own acculturization, want to study those mores that affect the community choice of musicians, if indeed the community has that option.[13]

The process of discovery is also facilitated by what may be called the oil-and-water process: just as oil floats to the surface of water, so talent emerges in the church if musical activities are made available to the constituency. In singing activities it is easy to detect the leaders; choirs and ensembles provide other opportunities for observation. It is important to be watchful for potential composers; these are usually well known, and only cursory inquiry may turn them up. Volunteering to notate the works of composers will also encourage their emergence.

Enlistment. If at all possible, training and enlistment should be patterned after existing practices in the culture and tempered by the constraint of Christ. Rewards are already practiced in many mission situations with hymn contests, performance of compositions, placement in a music office, and so forth.

A primary means of motivation is appeal. In some cultures, the missionary making the appeal will need to bear in mind the timidity either imposed by the culture or at least assumed for propriety. New converts, especially, respond if the role of Christian leadership is explained as a need not necessarily likely to frustrate the reticence required by the mores of a given culture (for example, of certain Oriental cultures). The role of sympathetic encouragement and even praise affords the missionary considerable opportunity to exercise imagination.

In countries with an advanced church development, such as Brazil, a primary need is the encouragement of a professional music ministry. Composers are emerging. Among Brazilian Baptists, for example, notable experiments with Brazilian idioms are being performed, and it is to be expected that this already flourishing field will mushroom with proper missionary response to the efforts.[14]

Training. We cannot train nationals in indigenous practice. We can introduce tools to increase their efficiency such as notation. While it

142   Music in Missions: Discipling Through Music

is true that no adequate notational system presently exists to record
many features of indigenous music, such as the various tunings and
other ways of thinking rhythmically, it seems highly impractical to
avoid notation simply because the Western system is inadequate.[15]
Practically, missionaries would find considerable difficulty in adding
an additional notational system to the one already known (which is
not in itself a definitive reason to avoid exploring the possibilities of
more exact notation). Even if music missionary specialists learned
another system, many missionaries and missiologists would not
know it, and communication in the mission world would face an
almost insuperable barrier. At present, it seems preferable to supple-
ment present staff notation with supplementary signs where feasible.
Even twentieth-century European composers developing new styles
and intonations not expressible within the traditional system have
generally preferred to continue to use it with supplementary signs,
such as a (+) or a (−) for quarter tones, or some other form of the
sharp and the flat.

However, if supplementary signs are incorporated into the missionary's notation, one must remember that they are not necessary
for the national. For example, if the upper note of a major third is
higher in the local scale, the national, one trained in the system or
at least experienced in it, will read it in that tuning and no other. A
supplementary sign, such as a (+), may be valuable to missionaries
as they are adapting to the new tuning or for communicating the
tuning to other missionaries, but it would be superfluous to the
national, who hears it no other way.

As church growth proceeds, there may come a time when training
will include procedures for promoting music in church, programming, and such subjects as voice. Here we must acknowledge a problem which has troubled music missionaries for some time. In certain
cultures, a highly stylized vocal production is associated either with
art or with dramatic musical works. Should singers be retrained according to European principles of vocal production? The answer will
depend on the effect of the native production on the voice. If it is not

Indigenization 143

basically a harmful procedure, and is bothersome only because it is "different," obviously it will communicate more effectively than a European style. The standard must be vocal health rather than preconceived ideas about voice.[16] Nevertheless it remains a fact that some of these stylized performance practices are positively harmful to the voice; in some cases, it is acknowledged within the culture either implicitly or explicitly. In these cases, it seems advisable to introduce as much corrective in voice production as possible while retaining those stylized elements (gasps, cries, groans) which can be retained without harm to the vocal mechanism.

Training will ultimately also include such subjects as music in the Bible, the practice of worship, and the contribution of music to worship. If the national believers can be led to formulate their own practices and approaches in a biblical framework, the practice will ultimately be more effective and attractive to nonbelievers.

The Bimusical Missionary

Missionaries are often astonished at the encouragement their attempts at language provide national Christians. In recent years, talented missionary musicians have discovered an even greater bond available through fluency in the national music. Just as missionaries normally have greater opportunity to become bilingual than field anthropologists, their opportunity to become bimusical is greater than that of many ethnomusicologists. They live continuously on the field over many years; their personal contact is deepened by the fellowship of the church; in short, their exposure to the second musical language is of quantity and depth not available to most scholars.

Perhaps the achievement of bimusicality by missionaries will complement the efforts of ethnomusicologists in a mutually helpful way: the ethnomusicologist, being a scholar, will continue to develop technique (especially investigative procedure) and to furnish in-depth analysis of field findings (which is not to deny one the privilege of field investigation). The missionary, on the other hand, living on the field for years and speaking their language fluently, will be in a

144   Music in Missions: Discipling Through Music

peculiar position to pinpoint differences in the conceptual processes of the two musics and to become a reporter of details and aspects possibly overlooked by a field investigator, whose time is likely to be limited.

The following steps are intended to be suggestive, and it is hoped that they might at least start a conscientious missionary on the road to bimusicality.[17]

1. *Learn to recognize and define truly indigenous elements.* This requires either natural or cultivated sensitivity. Be especially alert to characteristic (recurring) features of scale or mode, vocal quality, stylized mannerisms, relation of instruments to vocal line (where applicable), positions and manners of playing the instruments, subjects of folk song, categories of music, differences in application (function) of the various kinds of songs, and subtleties of text-and-music relationships.[18]

2. *Study the changes naturally introduced into Western songs, if any of these are sung.* Some of these will be obvious: a tune made pentatonic by the duplication of melody notes bordering the tritone in the diatonic scale, rhythmic variations to conform to a popular local meter, glissandi, and so forth. Try to anticipate what would be done in a given situation or melody. Incidentally, very little singing in other nations, even of the same hymns, is as fast as it generally is in America.

3. *Memorize and study melodies associated with various life activities: working, marrying, initiation, and* the like. A tape recorder is indispensable. Try to learn from informants which melodies are most characteristic of given activities; concentrate on those which reveal the most.

4. *Take lessons or enroll in private study.* This is easier in the high cultures such as Japan where teachers are recognized in the economic structure, but it is possible virtually anywhere. I have heard Americans apparently fluent on the African finger piano, so common across much of East and South Africa.

5. *Attempt to discover the conceptual process in which music is heard.* It is dangerous to generalize, of course, but it is also important to start somewhere, so Figures 1 and 2 have been given to contrast in a very

Indigenization

general way certain basic aspects of musical perception which might

	European—American	Indian
	1. Intensity - relaxation (tension - resolution).	1. Static.
Conceptual Processes	2. Dynamic - sense of progression (almost every note has some kind of tendency.	2. Coloristic - generally controlled and dominated by a single idea. The music is not becoming, it *is*.
	3. Characterized by presence of energy - accumulation and release.	3. Listener is in role of detachment, observation.
	4. Tonicity.	4. Tonality without such strong domination of one tonic.
Musical Elements	5. Diatonic (7 note).	5. Pentatonic, exotic scales, or modal.
	6. Development (in technical sense).	6. Highly patterned (modes) virtuosic and highly embellished.
Performance	7. Strong relationship to printed page.	7. Improvisatory.

Figure 1. Conceptual processes in Western and Indian music.

146   Music in Missions: Discipling Through Music

help a beginner "get a handle" on contrasting conceptual processes in music.

Figure 1. Functional harmony as evolved in the seventeenth and eighteenth centuries in Europe is essentially a process of building intensity or tension, primarily through dissonance, and resolving it by an appropriate consonance. The first four measures of Beethoven's Third Symphony (*Eroica*), for example, establish the tonic chord through an orchestral background to an arpeggiated bass melody that consists only of tonic-chord notes; in measure five, the melody moves to a C sharp, a tense nonkey note which requires relaxation through resolution to a D within a G-minor chord in the six-four position (which, in turn, resolves to a D-major chord: its own dominant).

In contrast with this, Indian (and much Oriental) music tends to be static, viewed in Occidental terms. If one listens to an Indian raga, it is the absence of tension (expressed harmonically although melodic tension is evident in the voice) and the interest in the inflections of the mode that place it in a very different kind of conceptual framework from, say, a Bach chorale.[19]

Thus, Indian music is coloristic and descriptive rather than dynamic. In diatonic music, almost every note has some kind of tendency, while Oriental music lacks that kind of tension. In Western music, there will be alternating periods of climax, development, and ease while Indian music will tend to be dominated by a single idea.[20]

Much Western music (meaning here, German functional harmony, not post-Debussy with his influence bringing Oriental concepts into Western art music) is characterized by the presence of energy, its accumulation and release, patterned in conventional molds (forms) and harmonies. This would seem to be strongly related to the nature of Western society. In Indian music, the listener is in a role of detachment, of observation.

Musically, Western music is controlled by strong tonicity and is diatonic. Tonality tends to be expressed in Indian music without such strong domination of one tonic. Its structure derives from combina-

Indigenization 147

tions of melodic formulae, that is, modes, rather than from a scale as such. Other Oriental scales tend to be pentatonic or hexatonic. The semitone, so carefully avoided in the pentatonic scales of other world cultures (sub-Sahara Africa), is at times an integral and important part of Japanese scales. European music achieves length through development (*Durchführung*), while Indian music is a highly patterned and embellished statement of a given mode.

In performance, Western musicians attempt a close approximation of the printed page. (Interpretation does not normally approach the kind of musical notation-and-performance relationship found in the Orient.) Much Oriental music, on the other hand, is highly improvisatory.

Figure 2. Statements comparing African and European conceptual processes must again be suggestive and general with specific application varying very considerably from one area to another. Whereas in European life, music is something to *listen* to in a somewhat passive role, generally in sub-Sahara Africa music is thought of primarily as

	European—American	East African
	1. Music is something you *listen* to (listening is one of the primary values in Western culture).	1. Music is something you *do.*
Conceptual Processes	2. Music stands alone as an activity (value in itself—alone).	2. Music is one part of a larger activity (dance, storytelling, accompanying work, etc.).
	3. Text is basically related to (linguistic) meter alone.	3. Text is related to meter and (linguistic) tone.

	European—American	East African
	4. Text is usually limited to specific vocabular functions.	4. Verbalization may include rhapsodic elements without specific meaning.
	5. General dominance of tonal elements (orchestras dominated by melody and harmony instruments).	5. General dominance of rhythmic elements (orchestras dominated by percussion instruments).
Musical Elements	6. Diatonic, with a general dissemination of equal temperament.	6. Gapped scales (pen-(tatonic and hexatonic, usually with natural tunings.
	7. Fairly strict adherence to written or traditional versions.	7. Free performance.
Socio-cultural Factors	8. Large body of professionally trained musicians.	8. Generally performed by the folk, with specialists often having a tribal office of some sort.
	9. Classical history.	9. Folk tradition.

Figure 2. Conceptual processes in western and African music.

an activity—something you *do*. Music as an activity has value in itself in the West; in Africa it would normally be found as one part of a larger activity, such as dance or storytelling. Western texts relate to

Indigenization 149

melodies primarily in their effect of inguistic meter and accent while in African tonal languages the text strongly influences melodic curve. An American (or German or French) singer does not in art music depart from the text, that is, the text is usually limited to specific vocabular functions (with the interesting exception of certain contemporary innovations in popular music and, recently, in charismatic Christianity). In much of Africa, verbalization may include rhapsodic elements with no specific meaning.

In regard to musical elements, the most obvious difference, of course, is the dominance of tonal elements (melody and harmony) in European music as opposed to the dominance of rhythmic elements in African music. European is diatonic, usually in equal temperament; Africans often use gapped scales, with natural tunings. Again, the fairly strict adherence of European performers to the written score may be contrasted with the freer performance so often heard in Africa.

Sociocultural factors provide still another vantage point for viewing the role of music. In the West, musicians form a large corpus of professionally trained specialists while specialists in tribal areas are often designated as an assigned office, which may even be hereditary. The classical history of Western art may be compared with the folk tradition of tribal areas, passing orally from generation to generation.

These comparative charts are suggested only as general models and are intended not to be absolutes but rather to suggest ways of understanding the conceptual process in which music is heard in different cultures. The missionary will be able to produce more meaningful comparisons within the specific cultures of tribes or language groups. As missionaries attempt to articulate their observations of the cultural pattern, they will grow more fluent in their ability to understand and absorb culture.

6. *Study the cultural framework and music's situation within it.* The environment in which music is produced is as important as the music itself, if we are to understand culture. Are local elements different from the national? Are there "classical" and "popular" categories? Do people

150   Music in Missions: Discipling Through Music

sing together, in mixed groups, solos, or antiphonally? Does all music have some kind of text or textual background, or are there kinds of absolute music? Is music more often described as beautiful, or is it likely to be described as useful or good (appropriate)?

7. *Cultural adaptation is a part of the missionary's Christian service.* It can be anticipated and prepared for; it cannot be taught. The anticipatory prayer life prior to appointment is as important as any other preparation the missionary makes. We might almost suppose that the spiritual difficulties are at least as great as the technical ones. We are not to separate medium and message; grace and wisdom apply to both.

8. *Understanding, appreciation of, and the ability to utilize the best in any unfamiliar medium is most effectively developed by the acquisition of a technical knowledge of that medium.* The practice and performance need to be articulate, fluent, and idiomatic. The missionary should study, with native teachers if possible, the basic vocabulary, its ramifications, implications, and application. Ideally, one would learn to play a native instrument.

It should not be assumed that failure to achieve bimusicality rules out the encouraging of indigenous music. There have been cases where missionaries were able to function effectively even when they carried certain disabilities in the language. Any missionary can encourage national practices and national musicians. One can make certain checks to see if indigenization is valid and is working. Delbert Rice, himself an expert, found one of his major activities to be a nontechnical one: he thoroughly tested the reaction of believers to new Christian melodies as he was aiding in the development of iKalahan hymnody.

> When the Christian *dayomti* was deemed complete, it was mimeographed and presented to the local Christian congregations to sing. Response determined whether it would eventually find its way into a hymnal or not. If the new *dayomti* was called for frequently during periods of singing when the congregation met, or if people were heard singing it on the mountain trails or in the fields, it was listed as a success. If not, it must be considered as stillborn and buried regardless

Indigenization 151

of the amount of precious love and labor that went into its development and birth.[21]

The missionary musician is in a unique position to gain the hearing of unbelievers, and to fellowship on deeper levels with believers. A perceptive Brazilian missionary stated a number of years ago:

Our music is highly salted with African drumbeats! . . . When a national composes, it will be in the format of American or European hymns or gospel songs, obeying that beat and melodic framework. If he really warmed up like a good Brazilian, true to the rhythmic flow in his blood and feet, boy! It concerns me and has for a long time that we don't seem to have any music springing up out of deep spiritual experience.

I am not the son of a poet, or a poet, and have never been able to compose anything, but it seems to me that it most likely will be the disciplined expression of inner feeling. This we lack! Why, I do not know.

The poetic forms which come naturally to Brazilians (and we have highly existential poetry, right out of the deepest sentiments of life) do not fit our classical musical forms, and it would seem that most of their music does not. There are some songs of folklore which do. Somebody needs to come down here, either temporarily or permanently, and spend some time trying to sound out these two factors: indigenous music and the factor of music out of experience rather than formal composition.[22]

Notes

1. *Webster's New Collegiate Dictionary*, Springfield, Mass., 1977.

2. Donald Hustad, "Must the Aucas Sing Our Songs?" *Eternity*, Feb. 1967, pp. 51-52,54.

3. Lewis, et al, pp. 35-46. This extremely helpful discussion by two missionary musicians and a distinguished missiologist should be carefully studied by every serious missionary musician.

4. Lewis, et al, p. 45.

152 Music in Missions: Discipling Through Music

5. Mary Key, "Hymn Writing with Indigenous Tunes," *Practical Anthropology*, Dec. 1962, p. 258.

6. Lewis, et al, p. 46.

7. Lewis, et al, p. 44.

8. Delbert Rice, "Developing an Indigenous Hymnody," *Practical Anthropology*, May-June 1971, pp. 109-110.

9. James M. Riccitelli, "Developing Non-Western Hymnody," *Practical Anthropology*, Nov.-Dec. 1962, pp. 241-256,270. See especially pp. 247-250.

10. Lewis, et al, p. 40.

11. Riccitelli, pp. 254-256. This entire article should be studied carefully by every missionary musician, especially the pages cited. It now appears that tone languages vary among themselves to such an extent that much additional study is needed before definitive norms can be firmly established—a monumental task that will require the cooperation of linguists, anthropologists, and ethnomusicologists. Information is needed which will coordinate the corpus of national song with the language. Already considerable evidence exists that this coordination varies; not all tone languages require "exaggeration of tone" in musical settings to the same extent. Furthermore, the various ways in which tone is combined needs further comparison with the musics of a given people, including the effect (for example) of glides, the relation of the number of tones, which intervals can or cannot express tone, the size of the interval required, the effect of tuning, and even the probably complex relation of melodic curve and interval size to the possible tone combinations permitted.

12. Merriam, *The Anthropology of Music*, p. 124.

13. Two important chapters in Merriam on this subject are "Social Behavior: the Musician," pp. 123-144, and "Learning," pp. 145-163.

14. The brilliant young composer, Nabor Nunes Filho, to name one example, has produced anthems and experiments in Brazilian idioms that are very encouraging. Rolando Raganas composed Cebuano music which was well accepted in the churches of Mindanao in the Philippines.

15. Bruno Nettle, *Theory and Method in Ethnomusicology* (Glencoe, Ill.: 1964, The Free Press of Glencoe), pp. 98-128, discusses the problems of notation in connection with transcription. He quotes the stand of the "Committee of Experts" of the International Folk Music Council in a stance adopted in 1950: "A notation tending to mathematical exactitude must necessarily depend on physical principles and would therefore entail the use of signs intelligible only to the specialists" (p. 126).

16. At the 1981 Africa Music Conference, missionary Fred Allen reported that he once transported a truckload of Zambian nationals to a convention. On the night leg of the trip, the men sang all night while riding in the back of a truck in the open air; the next day at the convention they sang beautifully and lustily, without any evidence of vocal strain.

17. This book obviously cannot purport to be a textbook on ethnomusicology as stated in the foreword. If a missionary wishes to learn something of ethnomusicology, he might begin with the brief bibliography in footnote 5 of chapter 6, and follow as opportunity allows the bibliography of ethnomusicology from suggestions as one

Indigenization 153

reads, as well as the literature in professional periodicals and in the music industry. The possibilities of furlough study are unlimited. Vida Chenoweth teaches an ethnomusicology course in Wheaton College which is designed especially for missionary candidates and missionaries.

18. An extremely helpful model for melodic analysis is provided in Vida Chenoweth, "Comparative-Generative Models of a New Guinea Melodic Structure," *American Anthropologist,* June 1971, pp. 773-782. Her formulas have the advantage of showing graphically the most characteristic intervals and the manner of approach and quitting. She also treats in less detail characteristic rhythmic configurations.

19. A considerable discography of Indian music is available. To name one illustration, one might listen to "Palavi," in the Southern Bhairavi mode, collected by Alain Danielou and recorded in the collection: *Anthologie de la Musique Classique de l'Inde,* Paris, Ducretet-Thomson, n.d., under the patronage of UNESCO.

20. An articulate description of Oriental style is found in a description of the music of Olivier Messiaen by Cecil Smith in "Messiaen's Complex," *New Republic,* 9 Jan. 1950, p. 22: "A piece of music, [Messiaen] believes, does not have to go anywhere. It does not become; it *is* . . . The music is plainly intended to be timeless—an escape from the Western concept of progress and constant forward movement into a quasi-Hindu Nirvana, in which music is a state of being, and not, as we conceive it, a state of becoming." Much of this discussion of Indian music can be applied in some degree to other Oriental high cultures, with limitations that would become obvious with little study.

21. Rice, pp. 111-112.

22. Letter to the author from James Musgrave, 16 Mar. 1967.

Epilogue

Donald and Violet Orr were appointed in 1951 as the first official music missionaries of any agency; in 1984 they retired. The thirty-three years of their service embraced sweeping changes that they could not have envisioned when they went out to chart new territory. Several colleges, universities, and seminaries now offer courses in music in missions and in ethnomusicology for mission volunteers. Major hymnals in the world of mission have started including large numbers of indigenous hymns. Music missionaries have encouraged the use of indigenous music through contests, choir festivals, publications, and public performances of works by national composers.

> The development of organized music programs in many churches occurred in South America and the Orient. In Brazil the seminaries in Recifé and Rio de Janeiro were granting church music degrees regularly, and the demand for ministers of music was greater than the seminaries could meet. In Japan the minister of music was emerging as a church-related vocation. . . . Associational and national church music festivals became regular events on all continents.[1]

At the beginning of 1985, the Home Mission Board of the Southern Baptist Convention had recruited a cadre of workers in the Mission Service Corps serving in the United States in music missions. The Church Music Department of the Southern Baptist Sunday School Board has included strong emphases (classes, daily prayers) on music missions in each of the national Baptist Assemblies for a number of

Epilogue

years. The dawning consciousness of the role music can play in bringing the world to Christ and to His lordship is spreading through many churches, and churches themselves are using music to worship and evangelize with new fervor.

But the biblical purpose of music in church still remains hidden from the vision and imagination of far too many Christians. Its purpose is the glory of its Creator, and that can best be demonstrated in spiritual worship and disciple making. Musicians are disciples first, just as any follower of Christ is. They are not reformed performers or artists; they are new creatures, like all other new creatures, working in a new and borrowed strength and spirit. This book was written to present a vision to church musicians and to all Christians of the high and fruitful role music is to play under the leadership of the Spirit of God.

Rennie Ohtani summed up the reasons for the blessings of God on her service in the Oi Machi Baptist Church in Tokyo:

> What is the secret to the success [of the Oi Machi program]? I would have to answer in one word - *love*. There were four factors of great importance: 1) God led. It was his time, and his leadership. 2) The pastor's enthusiasm, spirit, and encouragement. 3) Musicianship and training . . . 4) People were willing to work. We chose Japanese to work through; we led them and expected them to do it. If they failed to do their work, it was not done - but this did not happen! In this way we taught them the importance of being dependable.[2]

Oi Machi is well known in Tokyo as being a discipling church. Their outreach during evangelistic campaigns has inspired many other churches. Part of the church's success, many believe, is due to a sensitive and valid use of music. The work of Ohtani produced national music leaders; many of them are still active in the same leadership roles after ten years. She recruited the support of the national pastor. She was not slovenly about her own musicianship. Above all, she drew the people of the church into a continuing love and service for the Lord.

156   Music in Missions: Discipling Through Music

Ahead lies the continuing exposure of Christians to the possibilities of music as a discipling agent. Many are yet to be called into this service. There is great need for specialized books on music in missions —books on the music of specific countries that might serve as a model for others to learn investigative techniques, books on strategies and techniques that have worked (or have not been useful), biographies and autobiographies of missionaries that explain how they used music, and so forth. There is need for more specific support from home churches for missionaries working in music.

Above all, there is need for the supreme weapon:

Prayer.

Perhaps that is why you read this book.

Notes

1. T. W. Hunt, "Music in Missions," *Encyclopedia of Southern Baptists*, vol. 4, (Nashville: Broadman Press, 1982), pp. 2361-2362.

2. Rennie Ohtani, "The Church Music Program," p. 7.

Appendix

Three Sample Code Structures

Code Structure on "The Four Spiritual Laws" ©

The outline is that of the tract, "The Four Spiritual Laws": (1) God loves you and has a wonderful plan for your life. (2) Persons are sinful and separated from God; thus they cannot experience God's love and plan for their life. (3) Jesus Christ is God's only provision for human sin. Through Him you can know and experience God's plan for your life. (4) We must individually receive Jesus Christ as Savior and Lord; then we can know and experience God's love and plan for our lives.

The frame given here can be presented as a choir "special" without extensive preparation, since these tunes are usually familiar. It is suggested that the piano begin each introduction *sotto voce* during the last few words of each Scripture; the progression should, at any rate, proceed without interruption.

This frame can be amplified by making each of the hymns a congregational song. Scripture readers might enrich the connotative value by providing a personal testimony in connection with each Scripture. Scriptures will be more effective if they can be given from memory.

A Canticle of God's Plan ©

Arranged by T. W. Hunt

Music in Missions: Discipling Through Music

Reader: For God so loved the world that he gave his only begotten Son.

Choir, in unison: His only begotten Son, Jesus Christ.

Reader: That whosoever believeth in him should not perish, but have everlasting life (John 3:16). Wherefore God also hath highly exalted him, and given him a name which is above every name: That at the name of Jesus every knee should bow, of things in heaven, and things in earth, and things under the earth; And that every tongue should confess that Jesus Christ is Lord, to the glory of God the Father (Phil. 2:9-11).

The Four Spiritual Laws. Printed by permission. © Campus Crusade for Christ, Inc. (1965). All rights reserved. Code Structure on "The Four Spiritual Laws" © copyright 1973 by T. W. Hunt.

Appendix

Reader: For all have sinned and fall short of the glory of God (Rom. 3:23, NASB).

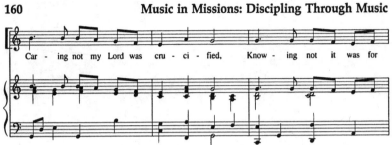

Appendix 161

Reader: But God demonstrates His own love toward us, in that while we were yet sinners, Christ died for us (Rom. 5:8, NASB).

162 Music in Missions: Discipling Through Music

Reader: But as many as received Him, to them He gave the right to become children of God, even to those who believe in His name (John 1:12, NASB).

Appendix

163

164　　　　　Music in Missions: Discipling Through Music

Code Structure on the Names of Christ

(A Complete Worship Service)
(Hymn numbers refer to *Baptist Hymnal,* 1975) Prelude

Welcome, Announcements

Offertory

Blessed Be the Name

Choir, Refrain, Hymn 50 (Repeated by congregation)
Leader: (Introduction) We're always giving people names: "Grumpy," "Sunshine," "Grouch," "Happy," and so forth. God knew this and placed great importance on names because names are an important way of communicating basic things about ourselves. God sometimes named a person before birth, and names were so important that He changed some of them: Abram to Abraham, Jacob to Israel, Simon to Peter, and others. The name stands for the person.

(The leader announces the title of each division, given here in capital letters and underlined.)

His Name Is "Excellent"

First Reader:	Leviticus 22:32
Choir (spoken in unison):	Our Father which art in heaven, Hallowed be thy name.
First Reader:	Psalm 111:9
Second Reader:	Psalm 29:2
Third Reader:	Psalm 23:3
First Reader:	Psalm 135:3
Second Reader:	Psalm 8:1
Third Reader:	Psalm 20:7
First Reader:	Psalm 124:8
Second Reader:	Psalm 72:17

Appendix

Congregation: Glorious Is Thy Name, Hymn 59,
                                 Stanzas 1,2, and 4

Glorious Is Thy Name:

Blessed Savior, we adore thee, we thy love and grace proclaim;
Thou art mighty, thou art holy,/Glorious is thy matchless name!

Refrain:
Glorious, Glorious, Glorious is thy name, O Lord! (repeat)

Great Redeemer, Lord and Master,/Light of all eternal days;
Let the saints of ev'ry nation/Sing thy just and endless praise!

Come, O come, immortal Savior,/Come and take thy royal throne;
Come, and reign, and reign forever, Be the kingdom all thine own!

His Name Is "Savior"

Third Reader: Isaiah 7:14
First Reader: Isaiah 9:6
Second Reader: Matthew 1:18-23
Choir: Jesus! Name of Wondrous Love,
                                 Hymn 74

Jesus! Name of Wondrous Love:

Jesus! Name of wondrous love,/Name all other names above,
Unto which must ev'ry knee/Bow in deep humility.
Jesus! Name of priceless worth/To the fallen sons of earth,
For the promise that it gave,/"Jesus shall His people save."
Jesus! Only name that's giv'n/Under all the mighty heav'n
Whereby man, to sin enslaved,/Bursts his fetters and is saved.
Jesus! Name of wondrous love,/Human name of God above:
Pleading only this we flee,/Helpless, O our God, to thee.

Third Reader: Acts 10:43
First Reader: John 1:12

166   Music in Missions: Discipling Through Music

Second Reader:	John 3:18
Third Reader:	Psalm 91:1,14
First Reader:	Malachi 3:16
Second Reader:	1 John 3:23
Third Reader:	1 John 5:13
First Reader:	Luke 24:46-47
Second Reader:	John 20:31
Third Reader:	Romans 10:13
Choir (spoken in unison):	JESUS CHRIST, SON OF GOD, SAVIOR! THE RESURRECTION AND THE LIFE!
(Each of these names to be spoken by individual choir members in rapid succession)	Dayspring from on high Light of the world Door Bread of life
Choir (spoken in unison):	THE WAY, THE TRUTH, AND THE LIFE!
(Individual members)	Our Passover The Propitiation for our sins Ransom Redeemer The Word of God Lamb
Women (softly, in unison):	. . . The Lamb that was slain.
Choir (Unison):	THE WAY, THE TRUTH, THE RESURRECTION, AND THE LIFE!
Congregation:	Down at the Cross, Hymn 454
Down at the Cross:	

Down at the cross where my Savior died,
Down where for cleansing from sin I cried,

Appendix 167

There to my heart was the blood applied; Glory to his name.
Refrain:
Glory to his name, Glory to his name;
There to my heart was the blood applied; Glory to his name.
I am so wondrously saved from sin,
Jesus so sweetly abides within;
There at the cross where he took me in; Glory to his name.
Oh, precious fountain that saves from sin,
I am so glad I have entered in;
There Jesus saves me and keeps me clean; Glory to his name.
Come to this fountain so rich and sweet,
Cast thy poor soul at the Savior's feet;
Plunge in today, and be made complete; Glory to his name.

His Name Is "Head of the Church"

First Reader:	John 16:23-24
Second Reader:	Ephesians 1:18-22
Third Reader:	Matthew 28:18-20
Soloist:	There is a name I love to hear,
	I love to sing its worth;
	It sounds like music in my ear,
	The sweetest name on earth.
Choir (sings	Oh, how I love [the Savior's name],
the refrain):	Oh, how I love [the Savior's name],
	Oh, how I love [the Savior's name],
	The sweetest name on earth.

His Name Is "Prince of Peace"

First Reader:	Matthew 19:29
Leader:	Acts 5:25-35,38-41
Soloist:	(Hymn 69, stanza 3)
	Jesus, the name that calms my fears,
	That bids my sorrows cease;

168   Music in Missions: Discipling Through Music

'Tis music in the sinner's ears;
'Tis life and health and peace.

His Name Is "Mighty God"

Leader:	Acts 3:1-8; Acts 4:5-12
Congregation:	How Sweet the Name of Jesus Sounds, Hymn 464

How Sweet the Name of Jesus Sounds:

How sweet the name of Jesus sounds/In a believer's ear!
It soothes his sorrows, heals his wounds,/And drives away his fear.
It makes the wounded spirit whole,/And calms the troubled breast;
'Tis manna to the hungry soul,/And to the weary, rest.
Dear name—the rock on which I build,/My shield and hiding place;
My neverfailing treasure, filled/With boundless stores of grace!
Jesus, my shepherd, brother, friend,/My prophet, priest, and King,
My Lord, my life, my way, my end,/Accept the praise I bring.

Second Reader:	Philippians 2:9-11
Third Reader:	And I saw heaven opened, and behold a white horse; and he that sat upon him was called Faithful and True, and in righteousness he doth judge and make war. His eyes were as a flame of fire, and on his head were many crowns; and he had a name written, that no man knew, but He himself.
The three readers (unison):	And he was clothed with a vesture dipped in blood: and His name is called *The Word of God* (author's italics).
First reader:	And the armies which were in heaven

Appendix 169

followed him upon white horses, clothed in a fine linen, white and clean. And out of his mouth goeth a sharp sword, that with it he should smite the nations, and he shall rule them with a rod of iron: and he treadeth the winepress of the fierceness and wrath of Almighty God (Rev. 19:11-16).

The three readers (unison): And he hath on his vesture and on His thigh a name written:

Choir and readers: KING OF KINGS, AND LORD OF LORDS.

Men: Anointed, Messiah, Christ, Immanuel, Advocate, Bridegroom, Head of the Church.

Choir: WONDERFUL, COUNSELOR, THE MIGHTY GOD!

Women: Vine, Teacher, Brother, Friend,

Men: Alpha and Omega, Rock, Bright and Morning Star, Hope, Servant, (gradually softer) . . . Righteous Servant, Suffering Servant.

Choir: Wonderful, Counselor, the Mighty God!

The three readers: Judge, Refiner, the Wisdom of God, Prince of peace, Son of man, Son of God.

Men: Physician, Shepherd

Women: The *Good* Shepherd

Men: (Gradually louder) Prophet . . . Priest . . . KING!

Choir: WONDERFUL! (Louder) COUNSELOR! (Louder) THE MIGHTY

170   Music in Missions: Discipling Through Music

GOD! KING OF KINGS AND *LORD OF LORDS!*

Choir and
   Congregation: All Hail the Power of Jesus' Name, Hymn 40:

All Hail the Power of Jesus' Name:

All hail the pow'r of Jesus name!/Let angels prostrate fall;
Bring forth the royal diadem,/And crown him Lord of all (repeat).
Ye chosen seed of Israel's race,/Ye ransomed from the fall,
Hail him who saves you by his grace,/And crown him Lord of all
   (repeat).
Let ev'ry kindred, ev'ry tribe,/On this terrestrial ball,
To him all majesty ascribe,/And crown him Lord of all (repeat).
O that with yonder sacred throng/We at his feet may fall!
We'll join the everlasting song,/And crown him Lord of all
   (repeat).

Invitation

Postlude

Code Structure on the Twenty-Third Psalm

The two prepared musical excerpts are examples of *Gebrauchsmusik* ("Music for Use"), brief musical statements valuable for momentary reinforcement of a single textual idea, without development or musical elaboration. Voice parts in *Gebrauchsmusik* should deliberately be kept simple, with minimum melodic movement. The reader should stand in front, and the choir at the side or rear, or vice versa (changes in the direction of sound act as a signal, and maintain attention). In reading, diaersis indicates a pause.

Reader: The Lord is my Shepherd,/I shall not want./He makes me lie down in green

Appendix   **171**

<table>
<tr><td></td><td>pastures;/He leads me beside quiet waters.</td></tr>
<tr><td>Choir:</td><td>"Come unto me, ye weary,
And I will give you rest,"
O blessed voice of Jesus,
Which comes to hearts oppressed!
It tells of benediction,
Of pardon, grace, and peace,
Of joy that hath no ending,
Of love which cannot cease.
    (1956 Baptist Hymnal, 227, first
    stanza)</td></tr>
<tr><td>Reader:</td><td>The Lord Jesus Christ, Son of God, is my Shepherd; He restores my soul. He leads me in the paths of righteousness for the sake of His own name.</td></tr>
<tr><td>Congregation:</td><td>Savior, like a shepherd lead us,
Much we need thy tender care;
In thy pleasant pastures feed us;
For our use thy folds prepare:
Blessed Jesus, blessed Jesus,
Thou hast bought us, thine we are;
Blessed Jesus, blessed Jesus,
Thou hast bought us, thine we are.
    (1975 Baptist Hymnal, 213, first
    stanza)</td></tr>
<tr><td>Male Ensemble:</td><td>I . . . am the Good Shepherd. The Good Shepherd lays down His life for the sheep.</td></tr>
<tr><td>Reader:</td><td>Yes, "though I walk through the valley</td></tr>
</table>

172   Music in Missions: Discipling Through Music

of the shadow of death," I will fear no evil. The Lord Jesus Christ is shepherding me.

Choir: (Choral speech) We beg you on behalf of Christ, be reconciled to God. He made Him who knew no sin to be sin on our behalf, that we might become the righteousness of God (2 Cor. 5:21, NASB).

Choir: (Slower and softer) "He made Him who knew no sin to be sin on our behalf."

Choir: (Sung) Well might the sun in darkness hide, And shut his glories in, When Christ the mighty Maker died For man, the creature's sin.
    (1975 *Baptist Hymnal*, 113, third stanza)

Reader: (Slowly) The Lord is my Shepherd. In the valley of the shadow You are with me. Your rod and Your staff comfort me.

Choir: (Choral speech) His rod comforts me. (Slowly, crescendo to the word *rod*) "And there shall come forth a rod out of the stem of Jesse, and a Branch shall grow out of his roots: And the spirit of the Lord shall rest upon him, the spirit of wisdom and understanding, the spirit of counsel and might, the spirit of knowledge and of the fear of the Lord," (Isa. 11:1-2).

Appendix

Reader: "He Himself bore our sins in His body on the cross, that we might die to sin and live to righteousness; for by His wounds you were healed. For you were continually straying like sheep, but now you have returned to the Shepherd and Guardian of your souls" (1 Pet. 2:24-25, NASB).

Choir:

Like a shep-herd, Je-sus will guard His chil-dren; In His arms He car-ries me, shep-herds me, o-pens my heart to His love un-bound-ed, won-der-ful, deep and strong.

174   Music in Missions: Discipling Through Music

Reader: He bore our sins in His body on the tree. By His wounds we are healed.

Congregation: (Sung) Was it for crimes that I have done He groaned upon the tree? Amazing pity, grace unknown, And love beyond degree!
    (1975 *Baptist Hymnal,* 113, second stanza)

Reader: You prepare a table before me in the presence of my enemies; You anoint my head with oil, and my cup is running over.

Second Reader: The Lord is my *Shepherd.*
Third Reader: The Lord is *my* Shepherd.
Fourth Reader: The *Lord* is my Shepherd.
Reader: Jesus Christ is my Shepherd! "And [the angel] showed me a river of the water of life, clear as crystal, coming from the throne of God and of the Lamb, in the middle of its street. And on either side of the river was the tree of life, bearing twelve kinds of fruit, yielding fruit every month; and the leaves of the tree were for the healing of the nations" (Rev. 22:1-2).

Choir:

Sure - ly good - ness and mer - cy shall fol - low me, shall

Appendix

175

Bibliography

This bibliography contains only items actually cited in the text.

Articles, Tapes, and Monographs

Ayers, T. W. "North China Paragraphs." *The Foreign Mission Journal,* March 1908, p. 283.

Bagby, W. B. "Lengthening the Cords and Strengthening the Stakes." *The Foreign Mission Journal,* July 1904, p. 34.

Bickers, H. B. "Music from the Village of Bambo Nyalube" (tape recording with transcription in the library of Southwestern Baptist Theological Seminary).

Brazzeal, David. Missionary Newsletter, September-October, 1984.

Boyd, Glenn. "Indigenous Tunes in Swahili," *Missionary Notes,* No. 6, September 1975, p. 8.

Chenoweth, Vida. "Comparative-Generative Models of a New Guinea Melodic Structure," *American Anthropologist,* June 1971, pp. 773-782.

"The Children and the Gospel in China," unsigned article, *The Foreign Mission Journal,* October 1908. p. 126.

Cooper, June. "The Japan Music Year," report presented to the Conference on Church Music for Asia, November 1973.

Corbitt, Nathan. *The Kenyan Musician,* a continuing journal for Baptist church musicians in Kenya.

"Correspondence," *The Foreign Mission Journal,* July 1897. p. 47.

Bibliography 177

Dixon, Curtis and Betty. Missionary Newsletter, December 1984.

Edwards, F. M. "Itinerating in Brazil," *The Foreign Mission Journal*, October 1908, p. 113.

Houts, Carolyn. Missionary Newsletter, December 1984.

Hunt, T. W. "Music in Missions," *Encyclopedia of Southern Baptists*, Vol. 3. Nashville: Broadman Press, 1979.

Hunt, T. W., "Music in Missions," *Encyclopedia of Southern Baptists*, Vol. 4. Nashville, Broadman Press, 1982.

Hunt, T. W. "Music in World Evangelism," *The Commission*, April 1971, pp. 24-26.

Hunt, T. W. "A Musician's Response to World Missions." Chapter 6 of *Bold Mission Music Handbook: A Music Director's Guide to Evangelism*, edited by Dan Johnson, Nashville: Convention Press, 1982.

Hunt, T. W. "Witnessing through Culture," Chapter 11 of *Educating for Christian Missions*, edited by Arthur L. Walker, Jr., Nashville: Broadman Press, 1981.

Hustad, Donald. "Must the Aucas Sing Our Songs?" *Eternity*, February 1967, pp. 51-52,54.

"Indonesian Christians Write Hymns for Pocket Hymnal." News Release, Foreign Mission Board, Southern Baptist Convention, 23 February 1978.

Jones, Nita. "Korean Baptist Music before 1970." *Missionary Notes*, July 1977, p. 1.

Key, Mary. "Hymn Writing with Indigenous Tunes." *Practical Anthropology*, May-June 1971, pp. 109-110.

Lawton, W. W. "Correspondence." *The Foreign Mission Journal*, April 1897, p. 387.

Lewis, Elaine T., Riccitelli, James M., and Smalley, William L. "More About Developing Non-Western Hymnody." *Practical Anthropology*, January-February 1964, pp. 35-46.

Masters, V. I. "A Human Interest Story," *The Foreign Mission Journal*, March 1913, p. 281.

McCoy, Gary. "Music Mission Trends Among Korean Baptists," *Southern Baptist Church Music Journal*, January 1984.

178 Music in Missions: Discipling Through Music

"Ministering through the Media," *The Commission,* May 1984, p. 37.

Mock, Darrell. "Hymnology in Japan and Its Problems," unpublished monorgraph, October 1984.

Musgrave, James. Letter to T. W. Hunt, 16 March 1967.

"Music Missionary News," *Missionary Notes,* September 1975, p. 3.

Newton, Jim, and Creswell, Mike. "Ivory Coast: Where the Music's Fresh," *The Commission,* November 1980, pp. 27-28.

O'Brien, William R. "Music Missions in Indonesia," unpublished monograph written for the Music in Missions class at Southwestern Baptist Theological Seminary, 1973, p. 3.

Ohtani, Rennie Sanderson. "The Church Music Program at Oi-Machi," monograph written for the Music in Missions class, Southwestern Baptist Theological Seminary, 1967.

Orr, Donald L. "Music at Work on the Mission Field in Colombia." Report presented to the joint meeting of Southern Baptist Seminary faculties with Southern Baptist Sunday School leaders, Nashville, Tenn. 19 August 1965.

Orr, Donald L. Letter to T. W. Hunt, 7 September 1967.

"Program for December, 1902." *The Foreign Mission Journal,* December 1902, p. 191.

Riccitelli, James M. "Developing Non-Western Hymnody." *Practical Anthropology,* November-December 1962, pp. 241-256,270.

Rice, Delbert. "Developing an Indigenous Hymnody." *Practical Anthropology,* May-June 1971, pp. 109-110.

Sears, Mrs. Grace Boyd. "Pingtu Summer Bible School." *The Foreign Mission Journal,* October 1912, pp. 110-111.

Sedaca, Jorge. Circular Newsletter, April 1984.

Shepard, Jean. Letter to T. W. Hunt, 9 February 1967.

Simmons, Sandy. Missionary Newsletter, 12 April 1984.

Smith, Cecil. "Messiaen's Complex." *New Republic,* 9 January 1950, p. 22.

"Some Chinese Children." *The Foreign Mission Journal,* August 1899, p. 90.

Spann, Fred. Letter to T. W. Hunt, 6 October 1966.

Bibliography

Steele, Edward. Missionary Newsletter, 18 September 1984.

"Sunday, 3 P.M." (Report of the Eighth Annual Meeting, Women's Missionary Union, Southern Baptist Convention, Chattanooga, 8-11 May 1896), *The Foreign Mission Journal*, June 1896, p. 79.

Supplee, G. William. "Principles of Incorporating Music of Other Cultures in the Music of the Church." Paper presented to the National Church Music Fellowship Convention, Grand Rapids, 1971.

Sutton, Boyd. Missionary Newsletter, 22 November 1984.

Taylor, J. J. "Trophies of the Gospel." *The Foreign Mission Journal*, April 1912, p. 303.

Towery, Britt E., Jr. "New Songs of Praise." *The Commission*, April 1971, pp. 10-11.

Walker, Catherine. "Called to Pray." Prayer bulletin of the Foreign Mission Board, Southern Baptist Convention, 5 October 1984.

Workman, Gerald. Letter to T. W. Hunt, 8 January 1973.

Lectures

Allen, Fred. Guest class lecture, Music in Missions class, Southwestern Baptist Theological Seminary, 23 January 1975.

Balyeat, Kent. Guest class lecture, Music in Missions class, Southwestern Baptist Theological Seminary, 30 January 1975.

Recordings

Danielou, Alain. *Anthologie de la Musique Classique de l'Inde*. Paris, Ducretet-Thomson, n.d., under the patronage of UNESCO.

Books

Blacking, John. *How Musical Is Man?* Seattle: University of Washington Press, 1973.

Chenoweth, Vida. *Melodic Perception and Analysis: A Manual on Ethnic Melody*. Ukarumpa, Papua, New Guinea: Summer Institute of Linguistics, 1973.

Chenoweth, Vida. *The Usarufas and Their Music*. Dallas: Summer Institute of Linguistics Museum of Anthropology, 1979.

McLuhan, Marshall, and Fiore, Quentin. *The Medium Is the Massage.* New York: Bantam Books, 1967.

McCluhan, Marshall. *Understanding Media.* New York, McGraw-Hill, 1964.

Merriam, Alan P. *The Anthropology of Music.* Evanston: Northwestern University Press, 1964.

Nettle, Bruno. *Theory and Method in Ethnomusicology.* Glencoe, Ill.: The Free Press of Glencoe, 1964.